Contemporary
sociology of
the school
General editor
JOHN EGGLESTON

The sociology of
comprehensive schooling

CONTEMPORARY SOCIOLOGY
OF THE SCHOOL

PAUL BELLABY

The sociology

of

comprehensive

schooling

METHUEN

First published in 1977 by Methuen & Co Ltd
11 New Fetter Lane, London EC4P 4EE
© 1977 Paul Bellaby
Printed in Great Britain
by Richard Clay (The Chaucer Press), Ltd,
Bungay, Suffolk

ISBN (hardbound) 0 416 55880 1
ISBN (paperback) 0 416 55890 9

CONTENTS

Acknowledgements

This book was written at the instigation of the series editor, John Eggleston, and owes much (excepting its errors) to his constructive criticism. I should like to thank Methuen for their enlightened approach to the series as a whole, and their anonymous referee for useful comments on the first draft of the book.

I have drawn heavily on other people's research and have tried to indicate this at appropriate points in the text. Work of my own that is incorporated here has in some instances benefited from criticism by Royston Lambert, Marten Shipman, Colin Lacey and Ray Jobling, among others; and above all from the lively co-operation of many teachers and pupils in three comprehensive schools and the loving support of my wife, Barbara. My thanks are due also to Margaret Farrow who typed the manuscript, and to all members, family and friends, of the 'Old Grammar School Commune', who gave material and moral support during the writing of the book.

Editor's introduction

Sociology has changed dramatically in the past decade. Sociologists have provided an ever increasing diversity of empirical and theoretical approaches that are advancing our understanding of the complexities of societies and their educational arrangements. It is now possible to see the over-simplification of the earlier sociological view of the world running smoothly with agreed norms of behaviour, with institutions and individuals performing functions that maintained society and where even conflict was restricted to 'agreed' areas. This normative view of society with its functionalist and conflict theories has now been augmented by a range of interpretative approaches in which the realities of human interaction have been explored by phenomenologists, ethnomethodologists and other reflexive theorists. Together they have emphasized the part that individual perceptions play in determining social reality and have challenged many of the characteristics of society that earlier the sociologists had assumed to be 'given'.

The new approaches have had striking effects upon the sociology of the school. Earlier work was characterized by a range of incompletely examined assumptions about such matters as ability, opportunity and social class. Sociologists asked how working-class children could achieve in the schools like middle-class children. Now they also ask how a social system defines class, opportunities and achievement. Such concepts and many others such as subjects, the curriculum and even schools themselves are seen to be products of the social system in which they exist. In this study of the school we can see with special clarity the ways in which individual teachers' and students' definitions of the situation help to determine its social arrangements; how perceptions of achievement can not only define achievement but also identify those who achieve; how expectations about schooling can determine the nature and evaluation of schools.

This series of volumes explores the main areas of the sociology of the school in which new understanding of events is now available. Each introduces the reader to the new interpretations, juxtaposes them against the longer standing perspectives and reappraises the contemporary practice of education and its consequences.

In each specialist authors develop their own analyses of central issues such as poverty, opportunity, comprehensive schooling, the language and interaction of the classroom, the teacher's role, the ecology of education, and ways in which education acts as an instrument of social control. The broad spectrum of themes and treatments is closely interrelated; it is offered to all who seek new illumination on the practice of education and to those who wish to know how contemporary sociological theory can be applied to educational issues.

One of the most striking features of a growing number of contemporary educational systems is the comprehensive school. Well established in North America, more recently introduced in Europe, these schools aim to provide common education for children of all abilities and all social backgrounds. 'Sociological' arguments have formed an important component of the advocacy that has preceded them and the debate that now surrounds them. In *The sociology of comprehensive schooling* Paul Bellaby offers a sociological examination not only of the schools but also of the arguments. He traces the development of the concept of comprehensive education in modern western societies, and considers the political processes through which comprehensive schools came to be established. He uses previously unpublished research evidence to examine the remarkably different patterns of schooling which emerge within a comprehensive system. The book provides a new and perceptive view of comprehensive schools and the consequences to which they give rise.

John Eggleston

1

What is comprehensive schooling?

Most of this book deals with issues in England. It outlines the history of English comprehensive schools. It asks how far the intentions of reformers have been met inside the schools, and what is left unchanged by reorganization.

However, to understand the issues we must put them in perspective. It is in this spirit that sociological ideas and methods are used throughout the book. Sociologists do not speak with one voice. As in all subjects, different arguments issue from different premises. The author writes within a perspective that is basically Marxist.

England's experience is not unique. We can find parallels in other countries – especially in Western Europe. There are also instructive contrasts – with the United States and Socialist countries. Comparisons between educational systems prompt us to attempt to *explain* what countries have in common and how they differ.

This brings us to a further point. The pattern of educational institutions in a country is only partly independent of the wider society and culture. Changes like comprehensive reform have to be related to broader shifts in ideas and beliefs, in social relations and in economic structure. The concepts of reform may come from educationists and the will for reform from politicians, but these actors take many of their lines from prevailing opinion, and have to shape their parts in relation to others in society. One mistaken tendency, then, is to explain everything by the intentions of individuals or groups. Equally wrong-headed is the attempt to reduce reforms to simple causes apparently outside human control, like the growth of income per head or the rise of socialism. Society is a highly complex structure.

This being so, it would be surprising to find that comprehensive schools were as novel in what they actually did as some seem to suggest. In fact they are likely to be subject to many of the same social constraints as other secondary schools.

Comprehensive schools in England

There are many questions to ask about comprehensive schooling, but first we must discuss the meaning of the term.

In England, its most concrete meaning is the abolition of the selection of children at 11-plus for separate grammar and secondary modern schools, and the establishment of secondary schools attended by children of all abilities. Soon after the 1944 Education Act, which made possible the extension of 'secondary' education to all up to fifteen years of age, a few schools were founded on the comprehensive model, but most were either grammar schools selecting the top 20 per cent at eleven, or the new secondary moderns who received the remainder. Within the broad national picture, there were many local variations. In some Welsh education authorities, two in five children at eleven would be sent to grammar school; some English authorities catered for fewer than one in five. The influential Norwood Report of 1943 envisaged a tripartite system of selective grammar, selective technical and non-selective modern schools, each dealing with children of a different aptitude ('academic', 'technical', and 'practical'). While the provision of grammar school places was general, only a minority of education authorities established technical schools, chiefly in larger urban areas. Variation in provision was in some respects also *inequality*. The campaign to reorganize secondary schooling stems from the middle 1950s. The Labour leadership did not make comprehensive education firm policy until the early 1960s. But after it returned to power in 1964 (for the first time since 1951) it put pressure on local authorities to prepare plans for reorganization. Though apparently impeded by a period of Conservative rule (1970–74), the reform has in fact continued gradually, without state legislation to enforce it, since 1964/65.

The graph illustrates the progress of comprehensive schooling in England and Wales between 1950 and 1974, the last date for which statistics are currently available. Comprehensive schooling

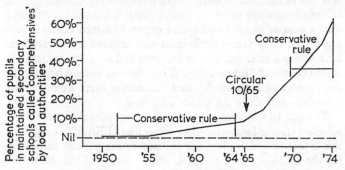

began to lift off during the Conservative government between 1951 and 1964, though it was not until the late fifties and early sixties, the period associated with the postwar baby boom or 'bulge' in the secondary school intake, that local authorities and the Ministry were prepared to extend experiments with this form of school organization. The impact of the Labour Government's famous Circular 10/65 is readily seen. Mrs Thatcher's much criticized handling of local authority reorganization plans between 1970 and 1974 (when she was Minister of Education in the Conservative government) did not seem to slacken the pace of reform. In the course of 1973 the halfway mark was passed, that is more than 50 per cent of children of secondary school age in the maintained sector were attending comprehensive schools (including a small number in middle schools of 10–13 age range).

However, the official statistics on which the graph is based have to be interpreted with care. In its survey of comprehensive

11

reorganization in 1971, the Campaign for Comprehensive Education reduced the official figure for that year (36·5 per cent) to as little as 12 per cent by specifying more rigorous standards for use of the term comprehensive (CCE, 1971). One and a half per cent in middle schools were left out. Schools in schemes that were still selective (for example at the age of transfer from the first to the second level secondary schools), schools that practised selection among themselves, and those that coexisted with grammar schools in their catchment areas, made up the majority of those remaining, and these too were excluded to reach the figure of 12 per cent in 'fully comprehensive' education. Even this exercise was not as rigorous as some might have wished. Comprehensive schools frequently (even *normally*) practise selection *internally*: only a quarter in 1972 had even a degree of mixed ability grouping in the early years, while most also selected for O-level and CSE streams after thirteen or fourteen and on entry to the sixth form (Benn and Simon, 1972). If one defined 'comprehensive' by the *absence of selection by academic ability* there would be few schools to include in the graph, even now.

The official statistics also conceal the considerable diversity of schemes among local education authorities (LEAs). Setting aside the extent to which plans are realized in the various authorities for the moment, there are three main sources of variation. The first is whether the individual schools cover the whole secondary age range, are part of a 'tiered' arrangement, or carry their intake to sixteen before sending some of them to sixth form college. The second source of variation complicates the first: it is the age at which secondary education begins. This was fixed by law until 1964 at eleven, but since that date some authorities have adopted 'middle schools', which span part of both primary and secondary ages − not the *same* age range, but either 8–12, 9–12, 9–13, or 10–13. The third source of variation is more subtle: it is how the authority allocates pupils to its various secondary schools. In many 'tiered' arrangements, *all* pupils are transferred from the lower to the upper secondary school at a single age, such as thirteen or fourteen. In some, however, it is only a proportion of pupils who are transferred to the upper school, the rest remaining in the lower school until compulsory leaving age. Those transferred may be determined by parents' choice, by the selection of teachers, or by parents in consultation with teachers ('guidance'). Transfer to the sixth form and to courses for formal examinations at sixteen is also done in a variety of ways, as we have hinted already. Further there is no standard formula for determining the intake into form one of a comprehensive school. It might be all pupils from a 'catchment area' or from 'feeder' primary schools. However, many authorities try to redress imbalances of ability between pupils in their schools by directing a few children from their local comprehensive to another that is adjacent. The combination of these three types of variation in schemes of comprehensive reorganization makes for a complex patchwork over the country as a whole. Having achieved a certain regularity after the 1944 Education Act, Britain's system of state secondary education is now as complex as that of the United States.

Some of the complexity will vanish when the full intent of Circular 10/65 is realized. For though Mrs Thatcher sought to remove it in 1970, the Circular was restored as the main guide to policy by the incoming Labour government in 1974. This document gave firm approval only to all-through schools (of 11–18 age range), and to tiered arrangements where *all* pupils transferred at thirteen or fourteen from lower to upper secondary schools. Since then schemes incorporating middle schools and sixth form colleges have become almost equally acceptable to the Ministry. But there is no doubt that any form of partial transfer between lower and upper schools, before leaving age, is seen as a half-measure which should be superseded by full transfer in the long term. Parents' choice between comprehensive schools near to where they live is probably becoming more not less common: it is institutionalized in many authorities, such as Inner London.

There are two reasons for the present diversity. One is the balance of power between central and local government. In law (that is currently the 1944 Act and the Act of 1902 which set up the local education authorities), the LEA is solely responsible for the pattern of school organization in its area. Its powers do not extend to determining the ages of compulsory schooling. Beyond that there is little that such an authority cannot do in the education of children. This was confirmed in the summer of 1976 by the Court of Appeal and the House of Lords in a dispute between the Minister and Tameside local education committee. It arose because the Conservative group that gained control in the May elections wished to restore selective education in defiance of government policy, and was ordered to retract by the Minister. The High Courts upheld Tameside's appeal against a previous Divisional Court ruling in favour of the Minister, arguing that Tameside had not acted 'unreasonably' in the meaning of the Act. Yet the gap between the law and fact is a familiar one. The effect of Circular 10/65 on local authorities is one illustration of the status that Ministerial 'advice' has in power relations between government which can change the law itself if necessary, and local authorities who depend on money voted by Parliament to carry out capital programmes. Even so, the party in power and the Ministry have to feel their way in relation to changing public opinion, and so comprehensive reorganization in Britain has been a compromise between the guiding hand of the Minister and the impulses towards reform or against it of local education authorities.

The other reason for diversity is that local authorities have in turn to compromise with the schools which are to be reorganized. British schools are not told what they should teach or how they should teach it. It is true that indirectly the work of the school is influenced by various outside agencies – the inspectorate, the Schools Council and the examination boards among them. Further, since 1944 all state maintained schools have had to accept whatever pupils the local authority has allocated to them. But the facts of life (and indeed Ministerial advice in the Circulars) have led local authorities to consult, especially with teachers, and to some degree with parents, before reorganizing the schools in a locality. The visible result of this level of compromise is that most authorities, especially the larger ones, not only differ from each other but individually contain a considerable diversity of comprehensive schools.

A bill is presently under discussion which will make comprehensive reorganization legally binding on local authorities. An Act of Parliament to reduce the present diversity of schemes (and of individual schools) would also involve a radical change in the balance between central government, local authorities and individual schools, in favour of a far more centralized system of education. That greater central control is in the minds of the

14

present Labour government is reflected in the Prime Minister's suggestion (October 18th, 1976) that a core curriculum should be laid down for all secondary schools.

As it is, local authority schemes are not only diverse, they are also in varied stages of completion. Of the 146 LEAs in England (excluding Wales and Scotland), thirty-six had reorganized completely by January 1974, but twenty-four had not yet started. However, ninety-two authorities in England were over the halfway mark: two thirds of the London authorities, three fifths of the provincial urban authorities (the County Boroughs) and 63 per cent of the Counties. Since April 1974 local government has been radically reorganized, except for London which was reformed in 1965. But there are as yet no figures for the period after local government reorganization, and it is convenient and less confusing to refer to the old pattern throughout this book.

In that great majority of the erstwhile LEAs which had not carried the reform to completion by January 1974, comprehensive schools often 'coexisted' with selective schools which took pupils from their catchment areas. This 'creaming off' was also conducted by schools that the LEAs did not control. England has a strong independent, fee-paying sector, which contained more than 400,000 pupils of secondary age in January 1974, approaching 10 per cent of the age range. In addition 122,000 pupils attended direct grant secondary schools. These had varying proportions of places allotted free of fees, which the LEAs usually funded and which were open to selective entry. However, the schools' main source of funds was a direct grant from the state. The LEAs had virtually no control over direct grant schools with a small proportion of free places, and very few such schools had agreed to cooperate with comprehensive reorganization. In 1975, the Labour government decided to phase out the direct grant, thus forcing the schools in one of two directions, either into the arms of the LEAs or into the independent sector. In the meantime a number of local authorities, such as Manchester, had ceased to fund free places at direct grant schools in their area. After 1975/6 LEAs will no longer be able to take up selective places in these schools. Though this will prevent the creaming off of bright children whose parents do not pay fees for them to be educated, it will not

15

prevent parents who can afford it from seeking schooling in the independent sector.

A further complication that cuts across many of those mentioned so far is the continued provision within English education for denominational schools, some of which receive direct grants, while others are independently governed but subject to some control by the local authority who 'aids' them financially. While this provision is small as compared with Holland, it remains, especially in the case of Church of England and Roman Catholic schools, a source of diversity in procedures for allocating children to secondary schools, and sometimes an obstacle to a fully comprehensive system. The Catholic Church has recently declared its intention to bring all its secondary schools into a closer relationship, at the level of organization and of curriculum, with the state comprehensive system. Hitherto, whether or not a Catholic school fell in with an education authority's plans for reorganization depended largely upon *local* negotiations. The position of Church of England schools remains less defined.

The debate about comprehensive schooling

The variety of what counts as comprehensive schooling in England makes it troublesome to define the term by pointing to an example. And so we shall have to turn to the *debate* about comprehensive education to find something approaching a definition.

To many proponents of comprehensive schooling, it is defined by the absence of selection; many opponents define it by the absence of choice. 'Selection' means education authorities' or teachers' allocating children to different schools or courses. 'Choice' means parents and children deciding for themselves what school they will attend or what course they will follow. It is obvious that restoring selection by educators is as much opposed to giving parents choice in their children's schooling as it is opposed to 'comprehensive education'. In fact ridding secondary schooling of selection is a *precondition* for complete choice by parents and children.

The authority of professionals and administrators has been called in question in recent years. Even teachers feel they cannot reliably select pupils for different courses at so early an age as

16

eleven. Yet every attempt to loosen control by experts and officials involves intervention by the state. In the English context (and indeed in most capitalist countries), the state is identified with uniformity, while the private sector is seen as the guardian of variety, whether in goods and services or in education. Not surprisingly, some critics of state control over education view the provision of all secondary education in one type of school as a reduction in the variety which is plainly *another* precondition of choice of schooling. They advocate wider access to the schools in the private sector. This can only be achieved by state funding of private schooling, whether directly or through 'vouchers' distributed to students (Boyson, 1975).

Most proponents of comprehensive schools seem sympathetic to enlarging the choice within education but feel it can be done inside a state maintained comprehensive system. They argue, indeed, that choice of curriculum can be wider in the one multi-function school than between schools which specialize in one type of course or another. Thus they look to the development of a series of 'options' around a common core of studies in the lower secondary school, and advocate 'open access' to the sixth form, rather than confining entry to those with enough O-levels to promise success in A-level GCE (Neave, 1975a).

This disagreement about whether choice can be provided *within* comprehensive schools or must be available *between* schools of different types is only part of the debate about comprehensive schooling in England. There are of course opponents of comprehensive schools who want a return to selection. It should be noted that there is nothing inconsistent in maintaining this view and at the same time advocating the abolition of private schools (Cox and Dyson, 1971; Cox and Boyson, 1975). Yet others point out that comprehensive schooling implies the extension of compulsory secondary education to more children and for longer: some are opposed to this (Illich, 1973). At the same time, there is scope for disagreement among people who *favour* comprehensive schooling about how much selection is consistent with the principle. It is to this aspect of the debate that we now turn.

Even within the most fully comprehensive local authorities at present there is some selection for special schooling. This is for children with a variety of handicaps, some specific some rather ambiguous, ranging from deafness to 'maladjustment' and 'educational subnormality'. It could be argued that the comprehensive principle requires that at least some of these children are catered for in the common school, that it would benefit them and other pupils (Anderson, 1973). On the other hand, their separation might sometimes be justified by the cost of the facilities they need and the economy of concentrating these in, say, one place for each local authority. Another embarrassment, however, is that the chances of being selected for special schooling are probably far from standardized: for example ESN (Educationally Sub-Normal) means a certain IQ score in one authority, but a different score in another.

As it is, less attention is paid to this problem in debates about comprehensives than to the provision of separate schooling for the 'exceptionally gifted'. Some hold that no school can be comprehensive unless it is part of a system that prevents the creaming off of the most able to selective schools. On the other hand, in the struggle against the abolition of the direct grant from the state to what are often 'super-selective' grammar schools, it was sometimes argued that these schools cater for the exceptionally gifted and that to continue them is *not* a violation of the comprehensive principle, but a way of concentrating facilities that the comprehensives might not be able to supply. Here there is a clear conflict about the definition of 'comprehensive schooling'.

There are ambiguities about the *organizational form of a* comprehensive system. In one view it is the *content* of education in the schools, rather than the outward form, that determines whether comprehensive schooling is going on. For example, the preparation of separate groups of pupils within the school for different examinations at sixteen militates against a common curriculum, at least after the third year. There is disagreement about whether 'comprehensive' means 'in the same school' *or* 'in the same way', or more technically whether academic differentiation *inside* schools is consistent with the comprehensive principle.

Finally, while comprehensive schools aim to include children of almost all abilities, their success in doing so depends on their 'catchment areas'. Especially in big cities, the immediate neighbourhood of a school may be overwhelmingly working class or largely middle class; it may, as often in America, include a dis-

18

proportionate number from disadvantaged (or advantaged) ethnic or religious groups. Since there is a clear probability that children of more prosperous and more educated parents will be more successful at school, comprehensive schools which draw directly from their neighbourhoods may be far from 'comprehensive' in the range of ability among their intake.

It will be clear by now that there is ambiguity in the term 'comprehensive schooling'. First there are competing definitions. One extreme resists all academic differentiation: comprehensives cannot coexist with selective schools; and streaming violates the principle. The other extreme accepts a measure of differentiation between and within schools as consistent with a comprehensive education system. Clearly, for the more exacting definition of comprehensive schooling, the merger of grammar and (secondary) modern schools into a common school is a necessary but by no means a sufficient condition for comprehensive education. This brings us to a second difficulty. We have to look beyond the outward forms to the innermost working of a school to discover whether comprehensive schooling exists there (see also Marsden, 1971).

Arguments for comprehensive schools

All who favour comprehensive schooling are opposed to segregating the mass of children into schools that have different curricula – like the grammar and the modern – at the early age of eleven. But there are three types of arguments against this form of segregation. The same arguments are often deployed against other kinds of academic differentiation, like special schools for the disadvantaged or the exceptionally gifted, and like streaming. One of these arguments is explicitly educational, though it is based on social and psychological theories. The other two have a more overt social-cum-political content. It is not uncommon to find two or even three of the views put by the same person. Indeed they are not necessarily inconsistent. But it clarifies the issue to separate them (Simon, 1970).

At its face value, the educational argument is that early selection – the 11-plus for example – does not allow for 'late developers'. These late developers can become trapped if they fail 11-plus and must follow a course that is not of the same content or at the same level as the one their latent ability calls for. It was customary to allow transfer between grammar and modern schools up to thirteen, but organizational rigidities appeared to inhibit such transfer. The comprehensive school is, or should be sufficiently flexible to allow late developers, and everyone else, to find the subjects and the level of study appropriate to their unfolding abilities.

The psychology that underlies this argument is a criticism of the use educationists made of mental testing. Between the wars some psychologists believed they had identified a component in mental performances that was scaleable, such that everyone could be ranked relative to everyone else by his 'general ability' or 'IQ'. Educationists saw this as an objective way of allocating pupils to different types of school. However, IQ is not a measure of specific aptitudes for academic as opposed to technical courses, or for these two rather than a course with a more practical and vocational bent. Further, the tests are not as reliable as a ruler with feet and inches marked on it. The same test can give different scores for the same person; different tests will give somewhat variable results. Finally, while most tests will give a high proportion of those tested the same rank in relation to others from one year to the next, there are individuals for whom IQ can change quite sharply in either direction as they grow older. For all these reasons the IQ test is subject to error and clearly should not be used to allocate children to different courses *if the decision is irrevocable* (Vernon, 1956).

It is clear that there is a basis for the 'educational' argument in psychology, but it may seem tendentious to argue that social theory lurks below as well. The theory is usually taken for granted. It only emerges when one asks: 'Why try to develop everyone's abilities to the full?' There are two possible answers: the first sees education as a source of individual fulfilment; the second interprets schooling as an avenue to jobs, and therefore a source of skilled manpower for society, and prestige and income for individuals.

Professional educators are more likely to give the first answer than are parents or pupils. If it is followed logically, education should be 'general' rather than 'vocational' and the content for each person should be determined either by the development of *his* interests or by a classical definition of culture. This point of view is common to 'progressivism' and 'traditionalism'. It is a *social* theory because it believes that the life that people lead outside school can be enriched by education. This is by no means self-evident. Indeed one of the prevailing questions within progressivism is how relevant schooling should be to the specific demands society will make on the child.

If schooling is seen as an avenue to jobs, then *comprehensive* schooling will be justified by the 'equality of opportunity' it provides. 'Equality of opportunity' will imply that there has to be a division of labour in society, and that certain inequalities of power and rewards must stem from this, but that it is *unfair* if the 'best jobs' go to the sons of well connected fathers, to those who have been bought a good education or indeed to anyone who has no proven ability and merit. Educators can sort out who has the ability and merit to get to the top. The school must therefore be an efficient and scrupulously fair means of sorting the sheep from the goats. This may mean deferring selection as long as possible, or even allowing the most able to emerge in open contest.

The social theory in the other two arguments for comprehensive schooling is much closer to the surface. One of these has been called 'egalitarian'. One of the motives behind the extension of secondary education to all, the abolition of fee-paying in County grammar schools and the introduction of an almost standard competitive examination for entry to these schools at 11-plus, was to give working class children an equal chance of the best education. A series of sociological studies in the 1950s and early 1960s showed beyond reasonable doubt that the middle classes still had far more places at grammar school than their numbers in the population would lead one to expect (Little and Westergaard, 1964). More fundamentally the studies pointed to various features of working class upbringing – material conditions, attitudes and expectations, language – which might militate against these children at school. Comprehensive schooling is sometimes seen as one way of diminishing these inequalities. It is supposed that a school that is socially mixed and has a fair share of equipment and skilled teachers, will be less likely to reinforce the disadvantages of working class upbringing than a secondary modern school which is overwhelmingly working class and is financed and staffed on a less generous scale than grammar schools. A rather

21

different version of the 'egalitarian' argument is that putting children of diverse social backgrounds into the same school and better still into the same school class, will make them more likely to mix with each other than if they are segregated by their education. Of course, the more long term expectation is that snobbery and conflictual attitudes in society will be diminished.

The third argument for comprehensive schooling is that a common secondary school can be the focus for life in a local community. It should do more than teach adolescents. It should be the local youth centre, the institute for evening classes, the sports centre, the concert hall and theatre, or anything that adult members of the community as well as teachers and pupils choose to make it. Cambridgeshire began this trend in the 1930s with its 'village colleges'. Today some plan to extend the principle to the city. Cities are not necessarily anonymous. In old working class areas and even in newer housing estates, there may be a strong sense of belonging. In any event there is a belief among planners and some social workers and teachers that it is possible to build a sense of community in areas where people share shopping facilities, pubs, schools and of course 'community centres'. As was noted earlier, in cities, and even in most small towns and villages, people tend to live near to others of the same social class or ethnic group. Such one-class residential areas are large enough in many cities to supply a whole primary school, often even a whole secondary school. The practical application of what we might call the 'communitarian' ideal for comprehensive schooling tends to collide with the 'egalitarian' and the 'educational' arguments, for it is sometimes impossible to achieve a balance of social classes or abilities in a school that serves a neighbourhood.

Some proponents of the community ideal are well aware of this. In fact they want to create schools where *working class* education can be perfected. They believe that most schools, including the comprehensives, transmit middle class culture, so that working class children are always at a disadvantage, and to succeed working class children must effectively become middle class in values and beliefs. This position takes us so far away from such common meaning as comprehensive schooling has for other educationists, that it is tidier to treat it as a general critique of the prevailing system of secondary education (Keddie, 1973). In fact

School Board elementary education (pre-1902), workers' self-education and some urban secondary modern schools are more of an inspiration to the contemporary working class education movement than comprehensive schools as others know them or indeed the Cambridgeshire village colleges.

If we add to these varying arguments in favour of comprehensive schools, two points of view from which they are criticized – the one in defence of selective education and traditional standards and methods, the other in favour of enlarged choice in secondary education – the debate seems very diverse, and the definition of comprehensive schooling seems as elusive as it was when we examined the patchwork of actual comprehensive organization in the country as a whole.

The changing polarity in the debate

But, the *actual debate* about comprehensive schooling is more polarized than this discussion indicates. Further, over the twenty years since comprehensive schooling became an issue, the focus of conflict has shifted and some people have moved from one side to the other. In the first decade it was those who wanted comprehensive schools against defenders of the grammar schools. Increasingly in the second decade the focus became the kind of comprehensive system we should have. Some people who had defended the grammar schools turned their attention to the curriculum of comprehensive schools. Differences among the early campaigners for comprehensive schooling which had been suppressed in the face of a common enemy came into the open in the second decade.

Two major reasons for this change must have been that reorganization was becoming a fact, and that the political parties divided on the issue. Many teachers were now working in comprehensive schools and trying to adapt their old approach to somewhat new circumstances. Few, if any, received formal preparation. Training college and university lecturers were usually even more in the dark. Thus no common philosophy took root. Instead, differences in approach, often between young and old teachers and in some cases between erstwhile grammar and modern school teachers, became magnified into doctrinal disputes when they were taken up by those who taught teachers or wrote books on education. The defence of traditional priorities and methods of teaching – a concern with the 'three Rs', belief in discipline, a preference for streaming – became confused with championing the 'grammar tradition' within the emerging comprehensive system. The progressive movement that had been at work in primary schools earlier was increasingly adopted as the banner of those who wished to carry the reform of secondary education further than achieving a common school for all in a neighbourhood. From about 1968, in the wake of the upheaval among students in higher education, progressivism became identified with opposition to authority, 'doing your own thing' and a new style of anarcho-syndicalism, the Schools Action Union. Most educationists who built doctrine on these trends were 'moderates'. Nevertheless they contributed to the impression that to champion completion of the comprehensive reform, to be progressive and to be left wing went together; to oppose any of these tendencies was to defend the 'grammar tradition' and to be right wing.

The two major political parties drove each other to opposing positions. Conservative Ministers between 1951 and 1964, especially Boyle, had approved (limited) experiments with comprehensive education, and a number of Conservative-controlled local authorities (such as Leicestershire) had pioneered reforms. Once the Labour Party announced its intention to press for wholesale reorganization, the Conservatives hardened their attitudes in defence of the grammar schools. The Labour Party's platform on education confused even its leader, who argued in 1964 that comprehensive schools were intended to bring grammar school education to everyone. But by 1975, the Labour Minister of Education was attacking the authors of the latest 'Black Paper' in defence of traditional positions, for being right wing extremists to a man: which was palpably untrue. Meanwhile the Conservative opposition moved from its rearguard position to an attempt to take up the initiative by making a longstanding champion of comprehensive schools, Rhodes Boyson, its spokesman and Shadow Minister of Education and encouraging him to develop the argument in favour of wider choice in education.

24

What the opponents have in common: a contrast with education in Communist China

In spite of the polarity there is already more common ground among the various factions in the debate than they can be aware of. Often when we examine religious disputes in the distant past, we are struck by how slight were the doctrinal points that separated the two positions. On closer examination, social and political or even economic factors seem more decisive than differences in beliefs. Obviously it is difficult to put the comprehensive debate in a full historical perspective, because it is too close to us. What helps, however, is to contrast the contemporary situation we know well from within with another setting. In that way we can get outside the English educational system and look back at it. The education system of Communist China is peculiarly suitable for this purpose because many features of it come as a surprise to Western observers, and because the Chinese have rather self-consciously set out to construct education that fits the proletarian revolution in China and is opposed to what they call 'bourgeois' education (Price, 1970).

Adult and child education in China is devoted to the reconstruction of the economic base, of society and of ideas and beliefs in tune with the ongoing proletarian revolution led by the Communist Party of China. The Party regards functional literacy as fundamental. Beyond providing this, the school plays a limited part in the educational process. The mass media – posters, film, radio, newspapers, pamphlets – and local groups committed to discussion and 'self-criticism' are major elements in what counts as *education*. The *school* is meant to be integrated with the mass revolution. Thus, since the cultural revolution of 1968, local *cadres* of workers and peasants have played a prominent role in its government, and also teach, though there are professional teachers too. The skills that are taught are intended for immediate needs. Students learn the thoughts of Mao, because they are as *practical* as technical skills in furthering the revolution. Those who persist in formal education must combine their studies with work in industry or farming, so as to resist the tendency for 'professionals' to become a separate caste.

It is difficult to transpose Chinese education into the language of English educationists. Note that there is no 'education system' in China – no set of institutions specifically committed to teaching and study, and separated from work, family and politics; and therefore no *system* that interrelates such institutions in terms of age-grades, levels (primary, secondary and higher) and means of access from one to another. The term 'vocational training', which takes its meaning from its opposite 'general education', has no relevance to China. Perhaps connected with these facts is that China has no period of compulsory schooling. What is more, the most highly schooled Chinese qualify less through examinations and similar 'educational' criteria than English students in higher education, far more because of their credentials as workers for revolution.

By contrast to China, England gives *schooling* a near-monopoly of *education*. Thus, where the family is encouraged to teach children, it is according to models provided by professionals like the paediatrician and the educationist. Television screens programmes that are specifically 'educational' both for pre-school children and for those in schools, child or adult (*vide* the Open University). Paperback publishers, like Penguin, distinguish their 'educational' titles from others, and, as a step in this direction, make some novels into 'classics'. Newsagents supply serialized encyclopedias according to the educational model. In this way, even where the school does not control directly what counts as education, it structures the efforts of others to teach their children, and to instruct the people. Not so in China: there it is agencies *outside* the school that determine the content of education – the Party and local *cadres*: and the school is subservient to 'the revolution'.

One impression that this comparison may give is rather misleading. It might seem that in England the school and the teachers are a law to themselves. This is not so. From 1870, both have depended heavily on the flow of financial aid and political will from government. The expansion of education and its reform have become issues in national politics. Schooling has been among the first victims of cuts in government spending whatever the party in power. Expansion or cuts, there has been pressure to model the curriculum to meet manpower plans. Further, the schools battle with 'non-educational' (even 'anti-educational') influences, such as 'rip off' films on television, commercial advertising and 'bad' homes, in order to defend their monopoly of education. There is a precarious barrier between the school and the world outside. Sometimes the school advances over the barrier to claim territory from industrial apprenticeships and professional training, or to assert control over the mass media. At other times the school retreats to protect 'general' education against the call for more 'relevance', or to assert 'academic freedom', with the accompanying claim that education is value-free, not implicated with religion or politics. Only medicine, in particular psychiatry, has a similar relationship to contemporary English society. In short, schooling and medicine alike enjoy *relative autonomy*: neither complete freedom nor total subjection to outside influence.

The explanation for this state of affairs lies deeper, for, whereas China has developed recently in virtual independence from Western capital and technology, England is enmeshed in international capitalism. For more than 200 years England's fate has been linked with that of other countries with whom she trades. Until the last quarter of the nineteenth century, England was the dominant force in international capitalism. She was pioneering production of consumer goods on an unprecedented scale in mechanized factories, and selling these and railways and machine tools all over the world. Schooling expanded rapidly – church and denominational schools, proprietary and endowed schools, the 'public' schools, new university colleges, professional training institutions. The state has intervened more and more as England has lost this position of dominance, and the United States, Germany, other Western European countries and Japan have become increasingly important industrial producers and traders. Much of the tone of national policy making in English education from the late nineteenth century comes from the sense that England must be schooled well enough to prevent her 'decline', and to keep up with her competitors. Thus, histories of modern education in England often start with the 1870 Act, that really did little more than fill in gaps in an already extensive provision of elementary education, as if it were the first step in education proper. By the 1970s that particular perspective makes far more sense, for the newest product of England's education, the

27

comprehensive school, is unequivocally a *state* institution. It has been forged, in part, in the anxiety that England might otherwise slip further behind in 'economic growth'.

Comprehensive reform elsewhere in Western Europe

Common secondary schools were an organic development from common primary education in both USA and USSR between the wars. Elsewhere in Western Europe, as in England, secondary schools came to specialize in academic studies and were 'exclusive', either in class composition or in selection by ability. Reform along comprehensive lines has been state policy in most of these countries during the last ten or twenty years. In each, what lay behind official involvement was the conviction that education must increase its output of trained administrators, professionals and technicians in order to feed economic growth (Poignant, 1969). This objective has been realized in various ways and to a differing extent (Council of Europe, 1970).

In Sweden, educational reform is centrally controlled. In the 1950s experiments were begun with comprehensive schooling in certain parts of the country and their results were monitored by university researchers. Somewhat before the results were clear, but in any event not without some encouraging findings, the government introduced the first phase of its comprehensive secondary school system over the entire country (1962). This consists of nine years of compulsory schooling, in three phases, each of three years, of which the first two phases cover common courses taught in the same mixed ability classes, and of which even the last phase is more than 80 per cent common. Thus from the ages of seven to sixteen Swedish children will normally share the same courses with the same classmates in the one school – the *Grundskola*. In the seventh and eighth grades pupils must choose one of four optional groups of subjects. Since 1970 a second language (English) has been compulsory not only up to the seventh grade as in the original plan, but until the end of the first secondary cycle at the ninth grade. The options are a third language, art, economics and technology. Whichever option the pupils choose they can still qualify for upper secondary schooling. However, in the ninth grade pupils must choose from nine

28

options, and this choice must to an extent predispose them to one of the corresponding four courses offered at upper secondary level, or else to the prospect of terminating studies at sixteen with one of the five optional courses that do not continue beyond that age. Until recently upper secondary courses were provided in separate schools, similar to the typically European division between parallel streams for all secondary education. However, the upper secondary school is now a common school *open* to all, though not compulsory and not attended by all.

From an English point of view the striking features of the Swedish system are its uniformity from area to area within the country, and the stress that reformers have placed on the curriculum and methods of teaching. The government has sponsored research and applied at least some of its results at all stages, and the reform *continues*, rather than stopping with the placement of all children of secondary age in common schools. The contrasts with the English situation are obvious after our discussion above.

Elsewhere in Western Europe reorganization often began with, and in some cases has proceeded no further than placing children in the first two, three or four years of secondary education in an 'observation cycle'. Though children are still transferred to separate schools at ten or eleven, much of their coursework is similar, and with the close of the observation cycle they may be reassessed and guided into different streams. In France, in 1959, following in spirit many of the recommendations of the 1947 Langevin–Wallon Committee, an observation cycle of two years was introduced. In 1963, before this reform was complete, the cycle was extended to four years. At the end of the observation cycle each child was assessed by a panel of teachers who advised parents as to the kind of school most suited to their child's aptitudes. Belgium introduced a similar scheme with a cycle of three years, while after 1963 the Netherlands began their reform with the one 'bridge year' after transfer from primary school to separate secondary institutions. Some city states and *Länder* in West Germany have introduced a *Förderstufe* or orientation period of two years. All these schemes have retained the system of parallel schools into which children are separated at ten or eleven. They have simply opened up the possibility of transfer between types of course, though rather more than the corresponding '13-plus' scheme in England, which in principle opened grammar schools to late developers from the secondary modern schools and also permitted transfer from grammar to secondary modern. However, even these partial reforms attend to the curriculum rather than, as in England, leaving the curriculum to the staff of each school.

From one point of view *Italy's* reform of 1963 already went beyond the point reached by the 'observation cycles', and subsequently some other Western European countries have trodden a similar path. Italy has been aiming at common secondary schooling since Mussolini, but progress was impeded first by the presence of 'all-age' primary schools, and secondly by a division within secondary education between more academic and more vocational courses. After 1963, all children who had completed primary schooling aged 11–14 (the legal, and in some areas scarcely factual leaving age), attended the *Scuola Media*, a comprehensive junior or first cycle secondary school. After fourteen those who wished to continue might, with the Scuola Media certificate, attend the *Liceo Classica*, which offered preparation for higher education, or one of a number of specialist schools (professional, technical, art and music).

The French introduced a similar concept in the same year (1963) – The *Collège d'Enseignement Secondaire* (CES). These schools were to be built for the purpose, starting during the fifth National Plan (1966–70). The CES is confined to the first cycle, and is a *multilateral* school. Its division into sections is reinforced by longstanding divisions within the teaching profession. Primary and secondary teachers are trained quite separately and have widely disparate status. Until the reforms primary and secondary education served children of overlapping age ranges (as in most of Germany), and they were administered by separate divisions of the Ministry of Education, a fact of considerably greater significance in the centralized arrangements of France than it would be in Britain. It remained true in the observation cycle, and even in the CES that separate sections were taught by teachers of different training and social standing. The Langevin–Wallon plan had envisaged a common first cycle manned by *lycée* staff. This is still not realized. However, the assimilation of various teachers and the reform of the curriculum are now being attempted within a common school.

Between 1965 and 1972, 1290 purpose built CES were set in motion and by the latter date more than three fifths of children in France aged 11–16 attended such schools. The pace of this re-organization exceeds that of England and Wales, which did not reach the halfway stage until 1973, three years after France. France's progress to date is probably only matched by that of Sweden (Neave, 1975b).

We have begun this investigation of comprehensive schooling with an attempt to establish the meaning of the term. Neither in the world at large nor in England by itself is there a uniform type of comprehensive education. There is so much controversy about the principles involved that we cannot look to educational writings for an agreed definition. Even so the contrast with China shows that trends in Western education (including here the Soviet Union) have more in common than appears at first sight. Common schooling at (first cycle) secondary as well as at primary level is now widespread. In some countries this consists of following the same core course in different schools (Germany) or sections within a multilateral school (France); in some (like England) of all pupils in an area being sent to the same school; and in an increasing number, of pupils following the same courses in the same schools (Sweden, USA and USSR). Furthermore the comprehensive principle is extended in many countries to the upper cycle of secondary education (again USA, USSR and Sweden, but also 'open sixth forms' in England). We must now ask *why* this trend has emerged, and try to explain its variant forms.

2

The changing face of capitalism and the emergence of comprehensive schooling

There are several ways of explaining educational change. One fastens on some aspect of present-day schooling, usually in the author's own country, which he wants to advocate or criticize. He will trace its origins and evolution, often with scant regard for the historical setting of the facts that are selected. Thus English comprehensive schools may be depicted either as the outcome of a long struggle by radicals for justice and enlightenment, or as clumsy destruction of an immemorial tradition of grammar school education.

A second method is more sophisticated theoretically. It hinges on the assumption that schooling responds to the demands of the economy for trained manpower, and has as its basic function the allocation of the right aptitude to the right job; the economy in its turn is driven by technical change. This 'technical-function' perspective is implicit in the argument that the reorganization of the secondary school is not only a step towards equality, but also *utilitarian*. Proponents of this view compare England with other countries, chiefly to show that England's schooling lags behind that of, say, Sweden, or even more typically, the United States;

what is more this backwardness is linked to our low rate of economic growth (see for example Benn and Simon, 1972).

Yet another, third, approach is to view educational change as the outcome of an ever-unstable struggle for power and prestige among different groups in society. In themselves, comprehensive schools are empty forms, made meaningful only by the often competing definitions given them by teachers, pupils, parents, politicians and administrators (Young, 1971).

This 'new directions' outlook is as *indeterminate* an explanation as the 'technical-function' approach is *determinist*. While it is true that educational change in England is the outcome of struggle rather than of technical change in the abstract, this struggle is not formless but constrained by a definite structure of human relationships – the capitalist mode of production. It is within the implications of this statement that we shall try to explain the comprehensive reform in this chapter.

Little enough research has been done on the internal working of comprehensive schools, especially in this country, but there is even less material with which to construct an explanation of the reform itself. When the government's moratoria on official papers have lapsed, and when a volume of intensive research projects has been built up – that is in ten or twenty years time – the historian will be able to give a more soundly based account than ours. But in the meantime we must act on our appreciation of the recent past, however ill-formed, and detailed studies must be guided by a theory of educational change.

Capitalism and education

One hundred years ago, no one could fail to be impressed by the capacity to generate wealth of a system of production which was based on the mechanized factory controlled by its chief beneficiary, the entrepreneur, and sustained by an army of wage labour. Today it is clear that science and technology are capable of serving more people more plentifully than they do within the constraints of *modern* capitalism. Vast material and human resources are caught up in the threat of war between 'Democracy' and 'Communism'. While one third of the world's population *wastes* energy, minerals and food, the two thirds which supply

33

much of these resources are on the verge of starvation. Even within the affluent countries, there are considerable inequalities. What ought to strike a modern observer as remarkable is the capacity of modern capitalism to overcome these contradictions, and to maintain its hegemony over Western societies, the 'developing' countries, and indirectly most socialist societies too.

As a first approximation to the complex relation between schooling and capitalism we may suggest that education helps explain this capacity for survival. What the factory is to the direct production of wealth, compulsory mass schooling is to the reproduction of the social relations within which production takes place (Althusser, 1972). The central function of the school in capitalist society is ideological rather than technical: it is to equip people to accept their roles, rather than to teach them skills; it is to sort out future factory workers, white collar workers and professionals and managers by their personalities and attitudes, rather than to allocate those with the highest IQs to the best paid and most responsible jobs.

Especially in the West, schools emphasize 'general' rather than 'vocational' education. Most people learn their jobs at work, not in school. Educational institutions respond in a cumbersome way at best to changes in the distribution of occupations (Collins, 1974). It is true that those who enjoy the high incomes of the top jobs usually have longer and more advanced schooling than others. However, it has been shown that in the United States only a small part of the inequality in incomes can be explained by years of education (Jencks, 1972). Further, while those with advanced education are generally of high IQ, among people of equal IQ longer schooling still appears to lead to higher incomes. IQ is even less of an explanation for inequality than years of schooling (Bowles and Gintis, 1976). The United States is well short of the 'meritocracy' that would satisfy the requirements of the technical-function theory of educational change.

On the other hand, schools devote intensive effort on a wide front to training 'leaders', dependable lieutenants, and a subordinate rank and file, and to determining, through what appear purely academic tests, who will fulfil each of these roles reliably. To this end, schools have different regimes for those staying on for advanced education than for those who leave at the compulsory school age. In England the sixth form gives more free time and more responsibility (e.g. as a prefect) than the lower school. Universities signal the assumption that they are preparing leaders by their stress on self-directed study and scope for personal development; whereas colleges of education and polytechnics, as if to train the lieutenants, have more contact with staff, a more detailed syllabus and a more crowded schedule. Almost all the people who emerge from these institutions will become employees or leave the labour force to be housewives, but by emphasizing the differences between levels in the hierarchy of occupations, schooling helps ensure that employees will not form a single class, and thereby preserves the dominance of capital.

How distinctive of capitalism is this particular link between schooling and society? First, note that in medieval Europe schooling was not confined to the age group we call 'childhood' (to which is usually added 'adolescence'). Scholars frequently entered university and even Latin grammar school as adults and were mixed indifferently with children. The lack of tie between 'childhood' and schooling reflects the extent to which medieval schooling had the relatively specific aims of promoting Latin literacy and the skills closely associated with 'clerical' occupations (that is, the Church, law, medicine and administration). By contrast, modern schooling is concerned chiefly with the *moral development of the child*, or, in other words, his preparation for roles in adult society (Aries, 1973).

The second comparison that should be made is with socialist societies, and perhaps also with the Third World. There are difficulties here. The modern Western model of education has been widely exported. Most Third World countries have education systems that reflect their colonial ancestry, or the present day intervention of Western aid and advice. Further, countries in the Soviet bloc have either (like USSR) imported or (like Eastern Europe) inherited a distinct preference for Western models of industrial technology, organization and management, and for rewarding workers according to their position in a social hierarchy of occupations, rather than according to 'need' or even to 'work done'. It follows from our simple model that Soviet bloc schooling will be shaped in ways not dissimilar to Western schooling by similar inequalities in the system of production. Even so, Soviet education has several features that reflect the central planning of its education with the guidance of a 'technical-function' theory. For example, two in three of university graduates in the Soviet Union are scientists or technologists, compared with one in four in the United States (Poignant, 1969). Another distinguishing feature of the Soviet bloc is that, while its schooling too is permeated with ideology, that ideology (as in China) is both egalitarian and emphasizes the responsibilities of the individual to society. It is an explicitly political ideology, in contrast to the implicit individualism of Western education (Bronfenbrenner, 1974).

The links our model suggests between capitalism and education throw doubt on the argument that *any* educational reform is purely 'utilitarian'. However, they are too stark to explain how comprehensive schools emerged, and the fact that secondary education takes different forms in different capitalist countries.

Schooling changes as a new mode of production becomes dominant (e.g. the factory supplants the farm), or as relations of production change (e.g. big business and the state replace the entrepreneur). The impact of production on education is twofold. First, schooling becomes the key means of social control with the appearance of the entrepreneurial factory system, but the modern capitalism of the state and big business requires changes in how this role is fulfilled. Secondly, changes in production alter the class structure: new types of people are exposed to education, and they seek to realize a variety of interests and values within it. Indeed mass education opens the school door to the conflict between classes. There is a further point: under capitalism, schooling has a somewhat privileged position, not unlike religion in medieval Europe, and its development – not just by teachers, but also politicians, administrators, parents and pupils – is partly independent of the mode of production. Often this 'relative autonomy' means no more than that schooling clings to the distinctive history – the 'cultural tradition' – of each country, which may be threatened by commercialism. In principle, however, education may develop in ways that *contradict* the mode of production, and thus endanger its stability. Whether it does so, depends on the outcome of the class struggle *within* education.

It is within a model of the relation between education and

capitalism, elaborated in the way these brief remarks imply, that we shall ask why secondary education has been reorganized along comprehensive lines in England. In this chapter we seek the social forces – the class struggles – that set the reform in motion. But they cannot be identified without comparing England's experience with that of other countries: the United States, Sweden, France and West Germany are given prominence here. The first step is to ask why comprehensive schooling emerged so much earlier in the United States than in England (and, of course in other Western European countries). The next is to compare the class structure of England with those of Sweden, France and West Germany in an effort to explain the varied outcomes of recent attempts to reform their systems of secondary education. In Chapter 3 the attention is wholly upon England. We ask how far and in what ways politicians and educationists, who actually planned the reorganization of secondary schooling, were influenced by class struggles. The reader will have no difficulty in recognizing that much of the ground that we traverse is in need of detailed research before our 'suggestions' are taken as 'findings'.

Why has England adopted comprehensive schooling fifty years after the United States?

The answer offered within the technical-function perspective to this question is that England has been slow to adapt her institutions to changing production technology and has paid the penalty in economic backwardness. It may surprise English readers that a similar argument was current in the Common Market in the 1960s, but that the then 'six' were comparing themselves *unfavourably* with England, as well as Sweden and the USA (Poignant, 1969).

(i) Nineteenth-century foundations

However, we can question this interpretation on several fronts. First, the introduction of mass schooling, at what we now call 'primary' level, was *also* earlier in the United States than in England, but until at least the turn of this century, England's economy was far more developed than that of the United States. In Massachusetts the mass school was introduced as early as the

1830s into towns dominated by the new cotton and shoe factories (Katz, 1971). Outside these towns, and even more so outside the Eastern seaboard, the United States was overwhelmingly rural or virgin territory (to Europeans). Within a decade, England was entering the first recession in which business rather than the harvest played the key role, and by 1851 more people worked in industry than on the land and in domestic service together. Yet England had to wait until the 1850s for a comparable development (the National Schools) and until the Act of 1870 before it was made possible to generalize mass schooling to the country as a whole (Lawson and Silver, 1973).

In the United States, the mass school emerged as a response to the intransigence of the industrial proletariat. Where, as in Massachusetts, that proletariat was overwhelmingly immigrant and of different religion and culture to the factory owners (Irish Catholic as opposed to old American Protestant), schooling had to fill the breach that in England was partly bridged by a tradition of deference to social superiors, by the control exerted by the working class family and by the discipline engendered by Methodism. Paradoxically the 1870 Act in England, and the subsequent development of elementary education by urban School Boards, owed much to working class initiative (Simon, 1965). In Massachusetts before the Civil War the initiative lay wholly with the middle classes, especially businessmen. However, by 1870 the working classes of the northern and midland towns of England were at once self-conscious and well organized, *and* substantially adjusted to the factory and to the 'self-help' ideology engendered by capitalism. A section of the working class sought 'opportunities' in education through reform.

The early mass schooling of the United States was also, to a greater degree than in England, *common* schooling. To explain this, we must compare the ruling classes of the two countries. The 1870 Act was a compromise between the Established Church, with its power base among landowners, and those who favoured a more secular education, predominantly Nonconformists rooted in the urban industrial bourgeoisie. The same split within the ruling class explains the 'elitism' that developed in English education during the nineteenth century. The industrial bourgeoisie had to match and surpass the landed aristocracy in style of life in order to achieve social and political equality. The reform of the 'public schools' ushered in by Arnold at Rugby in the 1830s reflects their demand to be taught manners, morals and leadership skills with which to combat the aristocracy on their own terms. For the English industrial bourgeoisie, schooling helped compensate for the absence of a thorough-going political revolution.

America had such a revolution in the War of Independence, though it was not confirmed as a victory for the *industrial*, as opposed to the *commercial* and *plantation* bourgeoisie, until the Civil War. Freed from the social and political hegemony of an aristocracy, the American bourgeoisie had less need of elite education than its English counterpart. It took advantage of its participation in mass schooling, to exert direct control at local level. The 1870 Act in England, and then the abolition of the School Boards by the 1902 Act, indicate that the English bourgeoisie had sometimes to use central state power to prevent the subversion of mass education by the working class or by the small group of middle class progressives who sometimes gained control of the School Boards.

(ii) *Developments in the twentieth century*

America entered the twentieth century with a common school, though access to education beyond it was a matter of privilege; England's education system was fundamentally dualist – on the one hand was a system of free (or nearly free) elementary schools for workers and the lower middle class, and on the other a system of fee-paying secondary schools, privately run, fed by preparatory schools and in turn feeding the universities, for the upper middle and upper classes.

It is in the period between the world wars and up to the 1960s that, at first sight, England seems to have diverged most sharply from the United States. In America, the junior high schools are established as neighbourhood comprehensives, while continuation to senior high school and higher education becomes so widespread, by degrees, that at the end almost half those leaving high school go to college. 'Progressivism' is the dominant educational doctrine. High schools offer a wide range of courses, many of them optional, which seem to allow the individual to tailor schooling to his own needs. In England, however, secondary schools become more and more academic. The sixth form emerges as a preparatory class for university entrance, and dictates the narrowly specialized character of studies further down the school. Most secondary schools are taken, in stages, under the control of local authorities, and are obliged to provide free places, until (after 1944) no state-maintained school can take fees. And yet a large independent fee-paying sector remains, and captures more than its share of places in the most prestigious universities. After the second war secondary education *in name* is extended to everyone over eleven. However, entry to the 'grammar schools' is by selection at eleven: only about a fifth are admitted and no more than a quarter of those will leap the next hurdle to enter higher education (Banks, 1955). The development of education in the United States seems to be 'democratic', but in England it is 'elitist'.

Persuasive though it may be, this account overstates the divergence between England and America in the last fifty years. In the two countries, capitalism was going through fundamentally similar structural changes. Control of capital became more concentrated, and the larger businesses went public, or in American parlance were 'incorporated'. With New Deal support, trade unions in America achieved levels of membership gained earlier in England, and in both countries trade unions were 'recognized' by employers and were assimilated into capitalism. The central state and local government played an increasing role in the economy and in the provision or control of health, education and welfare services.

It is true that in America common secondary schooling was developed out of common elementary schooling. But this coincided with the absorption into the urban labour force of groups hitherto outside the influence of industrial capitalism – small farmers, Southern Negroes migrating to the North, and the legacy of the waves of immigration that ended in the 1920s. *Common* secondary schooling promoted 'assimilation' to an increasingly urban and industrial work and living environment. At the same time the tradition of the common *curriculum* was put under threat, and remains under threat from pressure to educate separately those with higher and lower IQs. This corresponds to the fact that within the corporations and departments of government, the ranks of employees were swelled by people who occupied positions of control in routine affairs, though, like the manual workers they controlled, they lacked control over either the organization itself or their own destinies. To justify *their* position, by crediting it to their ability and merit, was to make capitalism itself seem a 'meritocracy'. *Inside* the American high school there emerged *tracks* and *streams*, in which students were separated to follow different courses. During the period dominated by 'progressivism', the practice in schools that prepared the proletariat was far from permissive and developmental (Waller, 1965).

Secondary schooling in England reflected similar changes in the structure of capitalism to those in America. We have seen that the proportion of pupils paying fees lost ground in most secondary schools: outside the most prestigious public schools, fee-payers had been small entrepreneurs and independent professionals for the most part. This 'petty bourgeoisie' was one casualty of the growth of big business and the state, to be found in England and America alike. Others were clerks and artisans. Clerks in small offices aspired to be managers or professionals, while artisans were their own men, if in a small way. In the last fifty years, artisans have faced extinction, while clerks have so expanded in numbers and have been so subordinated to routine and hierarchical control that they have faced proletarianization.

Proletarianization is the process by which those who have some autonomy in their work are absorbed into capitalist relations of production and reduced to collective wage labour. One tendency in capitalism is to bring independent producers and shop keepers, professionals and those who hold office, together with people who have special skills, to the position where they have no other means of support than to earn a wage or salary in someone else's employment, and where their jobs are so routinized and simplified that almost anyone can perform them. There is of course a counter-tendency for the work force to become fragmented and distributed in a hierarchy of prestige and authority. Consequently 'staff' whose tasks are 'mental' are not of the same class as 'workers' who do 'manual' jobs. And yet the 'new middle classes' are often threatened by absorption into the proletariat proper (Braverman, 1974).

41

In the case of clerical workers proletarianization is by now less of a threat, more of a present reality which has to be lived with. Between the wars it spurred a counter-attack, albeit of a characteristically individualist form. Clerks and artisans sought evening classes for self-improvement, and pressurized their children to gain scholarships to grammar school and bursaries to higher education. The developing academic curriculum of the grammar school reflects the ambition of such parents that their children should be 'professionalized' (Lacey, 1970). Unwittingly they contributed to the growth of those large scale organizations which have engulfed the clerk and artisan.

The comprehensive high school of the United States and the selective system of secondary education of England that emerged during the twentieth century and up to the 1960s are thus outcomes of social processes that have more in common than would appear at first sight.

The principal *difference* between education in America and education in England during this period was ideological: that is, it lay in what schooling was seen to be doing not so much in what it actually did. In America the ruling class has consistently justified its position with the argument that anyone can become president of the corporation or even President of the United States. Today the top positions are made to seem accessible to those of high IQ and educational attainment. If they are to appear *open* it must be because education keeps children's options open by delaying selection and leaving it to the student to drop out when he feels he has reached the limits of his ability.

This ideology of 'contest mobility' must be distinguished from the traditional English ideology of 'sponsored mobility' (Turner, 1961). This is a legacy of an aristocratic society. Access to the elite is like access to an exclusive club: one has to be co-opted or sponsored for membership by someone who can vouch that one has the right character and outlook. Because the habit of deference is more strongly embedded in England than America, the ruling class does not have the same need to make it appear that anyone can join them. In fact the English ruling class have been able to sustain the deference they enjoy by ensuring that new recruits have the same style of life and manner of self-presentation as they, acquired through independent schools, selective schools and elitist universities.

These differences in ideology have consequences for the way educational problems are defined on each side of the Atlantic. In England, most critics of the grammar schools saw them as middle class clubs and tried (by persuasion) to gain entry for ordinary people; the defenders protested as would members of a golf club if their greens were invaded by people with the wrong footwear. In America, however, the critics of secondary education treated the segregation of Whites and Blacks as the source of inequality and conflict, and saw in desegregation of the schools a way of overcoming racial conflict by encouraging healthy competition on 'equal' terms between individuals, regardless of race; those who defended the inequality claimed that it was based on inherited IQ, as if there was a fair contest already, but Blacks lost because they were lame. Comparatively few analysts in England or America have approached their problems in terms of the relation of education to capitalism.

What explains the emergence of comprehensive schooling in England?

In all capitalist societies, the growth of big business and the increasing intervention of the state have been associated with important changes in the composition of the labour force. It has been redistributed in two directions – first, away from manufacturing, mining and agriculture and into the distribution and service sector; secondly, out of manual work and into non-manual work. By the 1970s there were more people earning salaries than wages in the United States. Western Europe is perhaps ten years behind the United States, but is advancing in the same direction. Many non-manual workers are engaged in controlling manual workers, directly or through advising management, designing technology or keeping books. Others sell manufactured goods. Still others help reproduce the social conditions on which the capitalist enterprise depends, such as workers in health, education and welfare. However, there are wide disparities in the social positions occupied by non-manual workers. The most numerous groups – clerks and shop assistants – have converged upon the position occupied by manual workers. At the other extreme are doctors, especially consultants. It is in fact groups with a claim to specialized knowledge, which can only be conferred by formal education, that have expanded more rapidly than others.

(i) Technical-function theory

In France, Sweden, West Germany and England alike during the 1950s and 1960s these changes in the labour force were interpreted as a requirement of the further development of technology, and thus of the capacity to produce wealth into the future. Relatively few people were entering higher education; early selection for secondary school was one of the bottlenecks. In this way, the technical-function perspective offered a ready justification for building new universities, for expanding teacher-education and also for experiments with secondary education in order to find a way of expanding its output of qualified students.

There are several features of the changes in education that were actually introduced that do not fit well with the technical-function theory. The first is that while higher education was expanded with state finance and there was much talk of the need to train more scientists and engineers, in practice the demands of students and the values of university teachers (not always in harmony) did at least as much as the imprecations of policy makers to determine the pattern of studies in higher education. Secondly, in America as well as Western Europe, universities are heavily inclined to 'liberal' rather than vocational studies. This is in contrast to the Soviet Union. It is far from obvious that higher education in the West gives people the technical skills their economic roles will demand of them. It is arguable that even the vocational courses equip, say, doctors and engineers, for problems they will meet only rarely, and neglect those they ought to deal with from day to day. Finally, even if we were to accept that the expansion in higher education was demanded by developing technology, it is not clear that the move towards comprehensive schooling is geared to increasing demand for highly trained manpower. Secondary schooling is even less vocational than higher education. Further, if the preparation of the still relatively few who qualify for higher education in Western Europe explains the reorganization of secondary schools, why was reorganization not confined to expanding the output of the selective schools?

(ii) *Capitalism and comprehensive schooling*

While the expansion in higher education is outside the scope of this book, it may well result from the same combination of two, sometimes contradictory, sets of factors that explain comprehensive schooling. The first is the need of capital to retain control over its labour force. The second is the interests and values of groups within the labour force, whose position has been altered by progressive changes in the structure of capitalism.

The bourgeoisie has for long controlled labour by deepening divisions within society that were inherited from earlier times. Thus, it may be argued, the conflicts between Protestants and Catholics in Northern Ireland, between Blacks and Whites in the United States and between native and migrant labour in Western Europe, have all become subjects of a policy of 'divide and rule'. However, this solution to the problem of order is almost exhausted. A condition of the growth of the capitalist economy is that it draws more and more people into employment, and into the sectors where development is most rapid, notably the large organizations of private business and the state. This tends to obliterate distinctions that arise from the economic activity of many in sectors that are comparatively undeveloped (and usually underpaid), like agriculture, small-scale building and scrap-dealing. Other things being equal, the labour force should have more in common with each other. However, the social division of labour separates production and distribution, manual and non-manual, and even occupations within each of these sectors – the various trades and professions are set at odds with each other. The relation between non-manual and manual workers is particularly indicative, because it involves setting one part of the labour force over another. As we have seen in the case of America, a common school system, in which everyone feels part of the same community, but where social inequalities can be glossed over as the reward of academic ability and merit, performs the dual function of socializing everyone into the advanced labour process and preventing labour from forming a single class consciousness and organization. Nor should it surprise us if there are strong

45

tendencies within the common schools to differentiate pupils and put them under regimes that will prepare them to accept the various roles they will play in production.

Within this model of the functional relation between education and capitalism, the pressure to reform the selective system of secondary education in England reflects, at least in the last resort, the demand of an expansive capitalism for the willing participation of almost the whole adult population in the advanced labour process. But the capitalist mode of production is not an 'agent' with a will of its own: it is rather the framework of constraints within which people conduct their lives. As in the last section we must turn to class struggle to seek the mechanisms of change in schooling.

While the long-run interests of labour are diametrically opposed to those of capital, labour is so fragmented that these common interests are not realized. However, even sectional interests are pursued in contradiction to capital – union pressure for higher wages has been correctly identified as opposed to 'economic growth' (i.e. capital accumulation). So far as recent educational reform is concerned, we can find three sectional groups within the labour force which have particular significance: the 'new middle classes', who constitute at least two types of interest; teachers of low status within secondary education; and the working class. The new middle classes initiated the reform; it coincided with the interests of secondary modern teachers (or primary teachers in France and Sweden); and, once reform became a political issue, the working class became involved. We shall leave the third and last question to Chapter 3.

(a) *The new middle classes.* The new middle classes are a section of the labour force composed of non-manual workers in various positions of control in the process of production and distribution, or in the reproduction of the social conditions on which production depends. They share a concern with 'status', and enjoy or try to achieve a fairly homogeneous style of life, mixing chiefly with each other. Quite considerable distinctions within the classes reinforce competition for status, which can be improved upon both by associating with others of the same occupation, and by advancing individually through seniority or promotion. The preoccupation with status stems from the fact that the 'control' which new middle class workers exercise over others is rarely either material (e.g. money) or physical (e.g. force), but normally symbolic. Educational qualifications are seen as giving the holder credentials to exert symbolic control. The security with which this control is applied varies sharply and progressively from top professionals and managers to routine clerical workers and sales staff; so does level of education. Even managing directors in big companies are not immune to dismissal, but the threat of proletarianization which we mentioned in the case of clerks, lurks in the wings for the middle and lower echelons in the professions and administration, rather than at the top. Paradoxically, the attempt to persuade others that they are 'professionals' and therefore worthy of the respect given to doctors is strong among those quite seriously threatened – like nurses, local authority social workers and state-school teachers.

Not only is the position of the new middle classes dependent on education, but its vulnerability to changes in the economy, short term fluctuations and control from above or outside, makes them grasp more tightly at schooling as a straw which might save them from proletarianization. This, to many teachers, middle management, clerks, technicians and the like, is a basis for devotion to 'continuing education' (the refresher course, the Open University degree). The same people, as parents, have another material reason to be concerned about education. They seek for their children an education which may lift them to a more secure position or prevent a fall. By comparison, workers who have long been proletarianized come to see it as inevitable and demand little of or for their children. For those 'at the top', who are more secure and self-determining, it is either taken for granted that the children will proceed to higher education or is a matter of lesser concern. This explains the finding that it is 'lower middle class' parents who are most ambitious for their children (Swift, 1965), and that working class children who do well at school often have one parent who is or has been, say, a clerk.

(b) *New middle class interests and educational reform.* In the last fifty years, the proportion of the labour force who exercise some control over others, however indirect or slight, has increased dramatically. The fact that most of these people are doing work that is routinized and controlled from above in its turn, means that the tendency to proletarianization has *also* accelerated. As a result more and more people are seeking advanced education for themselves and their children, and very few can afford to pay for it. We have already mentioned the early pressure on the grammar school. The tendency to stay beyond the legal leaving age illustrates the same pressure: before the school leaving age was raised to sixteen in 1973, two thirds of children in maintained schools stayed at fifteen and one third at sixteen; whereas only twenty years before staying on was all but confined to grammar schools, and 'early leaving' was a cause of considerable concern even there. More significant still, secondary modern schools and early comprehensives led the way in offering O-level GCE studies (the grammar school intermediate certificate) to those who had failed the 11-plus selection procedure. Inevitably, 11-plus came to be seen as a bottleneck, blocking access to advanced education for the new middle class parents who sought it for their children and could not muster the pass-level. It is more than likely that the same pressure lies behind criticism of streaming practices inside comprehensive schools, and explains the prevalence of the 'open sixth form', which allows those who have fallen at the intermediate level to have a second bite at the cherry.

(c) *The class interests of educationists.* These changes are defensible educationally, but it is not necessarily educational reasons that impelled them. Even those who advocated them on educational grounds might have had sectional interests. Secondary modern school teachers had been offered the prospect of equal status with their colleagues in grammar schools by the merger of the elementary and secondary school systems in 1944. This equality did not materialize. And yet modern schools trod in the footsteps of the grammar schools – introducing O-levels and streaming in order to prepare the most able to take them; eventually pressing for another qualification more accessible to modern school pupils: the CSE (Certificate of Secondary Education). Secondary school reform realized the ambitions of many modern school teachers. It is true that the union in which they were most heavily represented (the National Union of Teachers – NUT)

48

maintained official neutrality on comprehensivization until it was clearly a *fait accompli*, and that the initiative in reviving long-standing debates on the common school (whether as multilateral or comprehensive) lay with renegade grammar school teachers who belonged to the union. But from the early 1960s the cleavage between modern and grammar school teachers – for and against comprehensives – became increasingly marked. Criticism of 11-plus was also a means by which educational sociology came to compete with educational psychology on equal terms; a very high proportion of sociologists specialized in educational studies, particularly in the 1950s and early 1960s.

(iii) *Class structure and educational reform in Western Europe*

The process illustrates well that educational change is not a direct consequence of the changing economy, and that it should not be interpreted at its face value either. We have given prominence to the structurally based interests and values of sections within the labour force who participate in education as parents or teachers, and mediate between the economy and educational change. This type of analysis can be extended to the reform of secondary education in France, Sweden and West Germany.

Sweden has moved furthest and most steadily along this path (Paulston, 1968). Secondary education of the first and more recently of the second cycle has been reorganized on comprehensive lines. Access to higher education remains narrow compared with USA or USSR, and teacher training is still divided in such a way that primary and lower secondary teachers have more in common with each other than with those who teach in upper secondary schools and universities. Of the four countries in Europe we are comparing, next to Sweden, France has done most to introduce common schooling at the first cycle of secondary education (Fraser, 1971). It has also carried out a rapid expansion of higher education, and has raised the status of technical studies. But the reforms in France have been firmly pushed by the social tensions that gave rise to the 1968 'Revolution', while those in Sweden seem at first sight another building block in the Social Democratic Party's construction of a mixed welfare-state/capitalist society, and to have been carried out step by step with research to test each foothold.

England's reorganization of secondary education lags somewhat behind France's and considerably behind that of Sweden. What is more the net effect of reorganization in the schools is far more diverse and ambiguous than in France or Sweden. There can be no doubt that the centralized policy-making and administration of Sweden's and France's education systems has contributed to the speed and extent of their reforms as well as to the more tidy and uniform appearance of the results in the schools themselves. In England, central government must compromise with local education authorities and LEAs must compromise with schools and parents.

In West Germany, the fourth of our European countries, the decentralization of education has been one factor in the relative failure of attempts to reform the secondary schools. Comprehensive schooling remains at an experimental stage, chiefly confined to providing a common core of studies in otherwise differentiated schools for part of the first cycle, and then only within some of the independent authorities (mainly the city states) (Heidenheimer, 1974).

However, central control is the instrument for reforms but not the motive force behind them. If we had been comparing the education systems of France and of England in 1950, we might have attributed the *rigidities* and *conservatism* in French schooling to central control. The real source of both conservatism and reformism lies in class relations not in institutions.

Much of this can be explained by the position of the 'new middle classes' in the various countries. Compared with white collar workers in the other countries those of West Germany have a definite status and are more distant socially from manual workers. For example, on qualifying secondary teachers in Germany become 'civil servants': this entitles them to considerable security in their employment and is a mark of respect in itself, though, like other people who are professionally qualified, they are also addressed by their occupation, in a way that only 'doctors' tend to be in this country. Divisions within secondary education correspond to status distinctions: the higher elementary school (*Hauptschule*) to manual workers; the classical secondary school (*Gymnasium*) to professionals and administrators; and the modern secondary school (*Realschule*) to intermediate non-manual workers. The expansion of technical occupations has been catered for outside secondary schooling as has much aspiration from *Hauptschule* pupils, by compulsory part-time education up to eighteen. The system of parallel schools is not challenged by tensions within the new middle classes, even from within the teaching profession, to the same degree as it has been in England, France and Sweden. Instead the status distinctions and the secondary school system reinforce each other.

If parallel schools and status distinctions reinforce each other, less marked distinctions between manual and non-manual workers should permit pressure to reform secondary schooling. But they will not *generate* this pressure of themselves. What may help generate such pressure are the counter trends within the new middle classes to which we referred earlier. On the one hand a large section of the new middle classes is converging upon manual workers: this is chiefly clerical and predominantly female. On the other hand, professionals and managers have increased greatly in numbers and enjoy a relatively high standard of living and social status. Their position is aspired to by the large section of the new middle classes threatened by proletarianization: it seems accessible only for the *children* of such lower non-manual workers and only through schooling. Since, in the relatively fluid status systems of Sweden, contemporary France and England, social aspirations are prominent and channelled through the education of children, narrow access to classical or academic secondary schooling will be seen as an obstacle to social mobility, especially by parents whose children fail to pass through by early selection.

Nevertheless, there are differences in the situations of the new middle classes in the three countries which may help explain the varied progress and style of reform within them. White collar unions are strong in Sweden, where, like manual unions, they are part of a system of central wage bargaining. Further, the Social Democratic Party has been in government from 1932 until 1976 not by one party dictatorship but by representing in its policies the diverse interests of many sections of the electorate. Thus new middle class interests are translated into educational reform by influence and compromise rather than through conflict. When one examines the research findings with which the government justified its decisions and notes that reorganization in full was set in train before the experimental period had been evaluated, one is convinced that the reform was no less *political* than in England. Yet the insistence on testing the ground 'scientifically' is evidence of the middle-of-the-road approach taken by the reformers.

The politics of France is less one of 'rolling reform' than of swings between extremes of democracy and dictatorship through revolutions and *coups d'état* that repeat themselves in a similar pattern. A strongly centralized bureaucracy maintains continuity in government. The top echelons of this bureaucracy in Paris are a meritocratic elite, selected for their posts after prolonged formal schooling and competitive state examination. They are beneficiaries of the selective schools. They also enjoy a good bargaining position as trade unionists, and are a left wing intelligentsia in the 'anti-clerical' tradition of the *lycées* and universities rather than right of centre generalists in the 'gentlemanly' tradition of the public schools and Oxbridge. White collar workers outside Paris, in lower echelons and especially in private industry, are far less privileged and both less well placed in union bargaining and less militant politically (Crozier, 1966).

In spite of France's turbulent politics, its social structure changed slowly over the twentieth century, until after the war, and more particularly during the last twenty years. Factory workers, drawn from the countryside and often Algeria, Spain and Italy, became mass consumers in the 1960s, and began to threaten long established status differentials between themselves and office workers and primary teachers. Similar processes were in train in England and in Sweden, though over a more protracted period. So too was the expansion of the top echelons of the civil services and of professionals in industry and public services. As we have seen the French government rapidly increased the output of students qualified for higher education from the existing secondary schools and established new university faculties in an effort to keep the boom in motion.

In so doing, we suggest, the government drew upon the aspirations for their children of the now threatened lower white collar workers, whose feelings of inferior occupational position vis-à-vis professionals and administrators were reinforced by the concentration of the latter in Paris and the antagonism between Paris and the Provinces. These aspirations were the seedbed of pressures for *reform* in secondary education to secure wider access to top positions than was possible within the selective school system. The same tensions translated to the children may have been a major factor in the so-called Revolution of 1968 which had as its main centre, Nanterre, the large *new* university faculty of Paris. While the left wing intelligentsia were divided as a group in their attitude to the student revolt, they were not by and large antagonistic to the widening of access to secondary education. Conflict has centred on 'standards' – upon whether the first cycle of secondary education can be entrusted to former elementary school teachers, or should be serviced by former *lycée* staff.

In England the class antagonisms generated by comprehensive reform have been somewhat sharper than in either France or Sweden. In no country has the reform been first and foremost a 'socialist' measure, in the sense that it stems from the labour movement and is a deliberate contribution to an alternative society. It is nevertheless attractive to the manual trade unions, or at least has become so since the reform was set in motion. It also attracts wide support among people who do not usually have an opportunity to say what they feel. The most conspicuous evidence of this trade union and popular support for comprehensive schools is in England, where in the last ten years the introduction of comprehensive schooling has depended to a great degree on the efforts of local Labour Party workers. Many of these are themselves new middle class; equally many are manual trade unionists. It is in England that the manual trade unions are their strongest as a political force in local and central government. But England's case needs more consideration. It is to this that we turn in the next chapter.

3

The politics of comprehensive reform in England

So far we have discussed the comprehensive reform in several countries without more than passing reference to who makes 'policy' and how. We must now turn to the politics of the reform, but it is so intricate that there is space here only for England. A recent study presents a more intensive analysis of English policy making than ours, but admits in conclusion that the politics must be set in a wider social context – that national leadership did not dominate events until 1964–70, and that even organized groups pressing for reform or opposed to it, were as much victims of social forces as part of them (Fenwick, 1976).

A question that is often asked is why the comprehensive pattern was not adopted when secondary education was developed after the war in England. Our model suggests that at first the grammar schools allowed the new middle classes to realize their aspirations; it was not until the late 1950s that staying on into the sixth form, the intrusion of O-level GCE into the secondary modern syllabus and criticism of 11-plus selection indicated the growing inability of the tripartite system to contain rising expectations. These underlying forces are reflected in a distorted form in the educational politics of the post-war period.

The closing years of the war were a forcing ground for seeds of reform in health, welfare and education that were sown earlier in the century. Educationists and politicians alike sought to extend compulsory schooling to sixteen, and to make provision for the secondary education of all over eleven. The main target was the 'all-age' school, governed by the Elementary Code, quite separate from the selective 'secondary' schools, and covering the ages of five to fourteen. There was little conflict over the objectives of reform. The main problem facing Butler, the architect of the Education Act of 1944, was to reconcile the religious denominations to losing control over many schools to local Education Authorities (LEAs). Butler's party, the Conservatives, ensured that not all schools under the state should prohibit fee-payers: the extension of the list of schools receiving a direct grant from the state, rather than being funded through and by the LEAs, was to form a bridgehead between public education and the still large and influential private sector. By comparison, whether the systems of maintained secondary schools envisaged by the legislation should be selective or comprehensive was scarcely an issue. It is true that a number of small teachers' and socialist groups had favoured *multilateral* schools since before the war (Rubinstein and Simon, 1973), and that even the largest teachers' union (the NUT) and the Labour Party had conference resolutions on record that advocated multilaterals. Leaving aside the fact that these proposals envisaged schools with distinct sides or sections, and therefore fell short of the ideals of many present day reformers, it remains the case that NUT was inconsistent in its advocacy of multilaterals and often sat on the fence, while the Labour Party in office (1945–51) – in spite of its huge majority in Parliament – did not oppose the development of selective secondary schools and even impeded some experimentation with comprehensive education.

However, the analysis of English educational reform cannot long remain with national government, the parties and organized groups; it must burrow down to local level.

55

LEA development plans

After the war, local authorities began to formulate development plans. The legacy of the past and their powers under the Act encouraged almost all LEAs to make use of the existing grammar schools and develop new modern schools when resources permitted. First, under the Elementary Code only the larger cities had built schools that could rival the grammar schools. These 'central' and 'technical' schools laboured under a disadvantage, because the more able elementary school pupils were attracted by the prestige of gaining a free place – 'winning a scholarship' – to study at 'secondary school'. When, after 1944, the maintained secondary schools came under the direct control of LEAs, most authorities had every incentive to concentrate the most academic teachers and the most able pupils within them. Secondly, the pressing need was to extend secondary education in separate schools to the 75 to 80 per cent of pupils who could not command a place in the grammar schools. If existing schools were to be replaced, it was the senior departments of the all-age schools that had priority. There was a general feeling that the buildings and equipment of the 'modern' schools should be at least as good as those of the grammar schools. Thirdly, for nearly a decade after the war resources for school building were very limited. Many development plans lay in abeyance until the late 1950s. Proposals for *experimentation* were viewed with scepticism.

An interesting exception is the proposals put forward in Middlesex (now part of Greater London) by the Labour group in control of the LEA from 1945 to 1949. They envisaged the absorption of grammar schools into neighbourhood common schools, but they faced the opposition of grammar school heads and the parents of grammar school pupils and found no encouragement from the Ministry of Education. The Labour group was dominated by a network of left wing teachers who were the chief activists for comprehensive schooling in London as a whole. In the event, their long term plan for comprehensive schooling throughout Middlesex was thwarted – the exception proved the rule of the day. Three experimental schools were established, no more (Saran, 1973).

Such ambitions had more chance of success in urban areas

which were so badly damaged by bombing that they needed rebuilding. Inner London, Coventry and Bristol were in this position. They did indeed plan for comprehensive schools. But at the same time they restored or replaced the buildings of many grammar schools, and established secondary modern schools to complement them. In Coventry and Bristol, comprehensive schools were confined to new working class council housing estates on the edges of the city. Even so, the more able pupils in their catchment areas were creamed off by maintained and direct grant grammar schools. Inner London, which was governed by the London County Council (LCC) until 1965, tried to distribute pupils of differing abilities evenly among their comprehensive schools, and yet a substantial minority of the most able was offered places at the grammar schools. It was therefore difficult in practice to differentiate a secondary modern school and a comprehensive school in these cities.

Outside urban areas the comprehensive school had a different, and usually more compelling rationale. We have to look to Anglesey in Wales and the Isle of Man to find fully comprehensive authorities before the millennium of 1965–75. These are thinly populated islands whose larger towns are far apart: given their very selective intake, grammar schools had either to provide boarding facilities or to be confined to two or three hundred pupils. Since grammar schools now sought viable sixth forms, and there was a low rate of staying on in the post-war period and the 1950s, it was hard to justify the staffing of a small grammar school. If modern schools had to be provided as well the diseconomies were aggravated. The comprehensive school was an economic solution which held out the prospect of developing sixth form studies for a small centre of population.

All the early comprehensive schools mentioned so far were 'all-through', that is they took in pupils at the statutory transfer age of eleven and kept them until the leaving age of fifteen, or beyond that in fifth and sixth forms until the age of eighteen. Most were purpose-built. Just as it was felt that modern schools should have a clean sheet, so the experiments with comprehensive schools were on a lavish scale. They were often show schools, and to have taught in them or better still managed them successfully was a stepping stone in a teacher's career.

For most authorities full scale organization along comprehensive lines was only possible if existing schools were combined and their facilities incorporated in new comprehensive schools. This was no easier from a practical point of view in the middle 1960s than it was directly after the war. The building of new modern schools considerably improved educational provision for the great majority of children, but it also established institutions with a different identity from the grammar schools, which grammar school staff might not wish to join.

In this context, the initiative taken in Leicestershire by the Conservative controlled council on the advice of Mason, its director of education, is of greater significance than experiments with all-through comprehensive schools. This 'Mason-Plan' envisaged a step by step reorganization of the secondary schools in the County using the existing buildings for the most part and preserving the main educational characteristics of each. The idea was to use modern schools as lower tier secondary schools which took everyone from a catchment area. At the age of fourteen, pupils could enter upper tier secondary schools if their parents chose, though parents were as a rule advised as to whether their children were capable of GCE work. The upper tier schools were based on old grammar schools. More recently the former partial entry to the upper schools has been replaced by undifferentiated entry. In this way Leicestershire was able to become fully comprehensive by the end of the 1960s, and even to incorporate all but one direct grant school in the scheme.

The politics of early experiments with comprehensive schools

Until the reorganization of local government in 1974, there were two types of Local Education Authority: there were County Boroughs (CBs), which were towns that for the most part achieved this status in the 1890s, many of them quite small; and there were Counties which corresponded to the ancient shires, and were often very large. Since the war, CBs, especially in the North and Midlands, have tended to fall to Labour in local elections; while the Counties have been controlled by Conservatives or (nominally) have had no party in control.

Let us take the Counties first. Up to 1962, when Pedley made a list of early experiments with comprehensive schools, twenty-five of the forty-six Counties had established at least one 'comprehensive' (Pedley, 1963). Only in four of the twenty-five had Labour held control at any time since the war; they were among the most industrialized Counties (Durham, Derbyshire, the West Riding and Lancashire). Labour had controlled two other Counties, but neither had a comprehensive school (Nottinghamshire and Northumberland).

The other type of LEA was far more often Labour-controlled, but less often took part in early comprehensive experiments. Pedley mentioned schools in only seventeen of the seventy-six CBs in his list of comprehensives. Twenty County Boroughs had been under Labour control without intermission between 1945 and 1962, but only two of them – Stoke on Trent and Coventry – had comprehensive schools.

It seems, then, that politics played a leading role only in isolated instances, of which Middlesex is one. An early generation of studies in the politics of educational reform in local authorities lends credence to this global interpretation. The analysts of Croydon's proposals for a sixth form college (Donnison, 1965) and of West Ham and Reading (Peschek and Brand, 1966) find the paid officials of the Education Office a more decisive element in the formulation of policy than party positions. Subsequent events have shown that this cannot be a general rule; rather, it reflects the lack of interest in education among local party groups on councils up to the early and middle 1960s.

Even so, the Conservative Party in government (1951–64), abetted by entrenched Ministry attitudes, developed a position towards comprehensive schools which was only hardened by the later Ministry of Mrs Thatcher (1970–74). Proposals for comprehensive schools from local authorities were turned down if they threatened existing grammar schools, and favoured only if there were large new populations to cater for or scattered rural populations. The schemes that advanced most preserved the essence of the grammar school, even if in the framework of a fully comprehensive scheme (Leicestershire).

The Labour Party and comprehensive reform

As we have seen the Ministry Circular 10/65, which required LEAs to *submit plans* for the reorganization of secondary education in their areas, considerably accelerated the foundation of comprehensive schools. For some local authorities the Circular was indeed a 'directive', and if they complied at all, they did so with reluctance; for others the Circular was 'permissive' – it allowed them to undertake reforms that were already planned. For the Circular was anticipated by growing interest in the issue in the late 1950s and early 1960s, not only within the national Labour Party, whose 1964 election manifesto was put into effect by the Circular, but also among educational administrators and teachers' organizations, and on both sides – for and against comprehensives.

In 1959 the conference of Labour Groups in local government was debating not *whether* to reorganize but *how* to make reorganization feasible politically. By 1964, the year in which Labour returned to office after thirteen years in opposition, a quarter of LEAs had radically changed their selection procedures at 11-plus and more than 70 per cent planned comprehensive reorganization (Rubinstein and Simon, 1973). A case study of local decision making at this time showed that in two authorities, Darlington and Gateshead in the North (and there is reason to think it typical) the Labour Group on the Council was persuaded of the need for reform, and, once in control, was acting in partnership with the Education Officer to prepare detailed plans (Batley, O'Brien and Parris, 1970).

There is, of course, a much longer history to the Labour Party's involvement with comprehensive schooling (Parkinson, 1970). The organization of teachers in the Labour Party (National Association of Labour Teachers) had campaigned from before the war, at first for multilaterals, and then in the 1950s for comprehensive schools in the more contemporary sense. They had frequently captured rank and file support at party conferences. And yet they had to wait until the early 1960s before they gained the centres of power even in most local Labour Groups on Councils, quite apart from the Parliamentary Labour Party. It was at this time also that the National Union of Teachers, the largest union, with its centre of gravity among primary and secondary modern teachers, began to debate the issue with a sense of urgency. The leadership came at first from grammar school teachers who had expressed their disaffection from the tripartite system by joining NUT. Opposition was hardening as well. Among teachers' organizations, the Joint Four, a federation of small associations largely confined to grammar school teachers, led the counter-attack, while there were rumblings of discontent within Conservative Constituency Associations at the reluctance of the national leadership to make the threat to the grammar schools a major public issue.

Comprehensive reform became an established part of the official policy of the Parliamentary Labour Party in 'Signposts for the Sixties', where it was one of five major themes. The decision to include it undoubtedly reflected the growing interest in reorganization among educationists and local party groups, but it had a wider significance. In the Election of 1959, Labour was defeated heavily and for the third time in succession. The party intelligentsia diagnosed the trouble as decreasing support for Labour from the working class, coupled with the expansion of white collar occupations who looked to the Conservative Party. It was assumed that the growing prosperity of workers had not only enabled many to buy their own houses and cars, but also changed their style of life and social aspirations: they now saw themselves as middle class, developed ambitions for their children, and changed their voting habits. If the party was to return to power, it must change its image: it must become a progressive party of the centre. Education was a middle class concern, and so it must play a prominent part in the new policy. However, the specifically 'socialist' aims of the earlier campaigners for comprehensive reform – to reduce inequalities and build community – must be relegated in favour of the need of a modernized society for more efficient use of talent, an aim that could only be realized by reorganizing secondary education and expanding higher education. At the hands of Harold Wilson who led the Party to victory in 1964, and again with a greatly increased majority in 1966, comprehensive reform was an integral part of the modernization of the economy and society, of the 'white-hot technological revolution' he pledged himself to promote.

The belief that comprehensive reform was a *popular* policy was shared by the Conservative leadership. In 1966 and again in 1970 (when to everyone's surprise the Conservatives won the election), Edward Heath avoided direct confrontation over educational reform. He did so at the risk of disaffection in the party rank and file, which expressed itself in the conference of 1967 where a ballot was forced after a substantial show of hands against the leadership's unwillingness to attack comprehensive schools, a rare event in that assembly. Heath's caution in campaigning was based on his interpretation of the opinion polls of the time. One poll (by Opinion Research Centre, published on June 30th, 1967) had been confined to educational policy, and reflected a large majority opposed to selection at 11-plus, and a large minority, concentrated among voters who were undecided between parties, who favoured comprehensive schools.

10/65 and All That

Circular 10/65 was one of the few pledges made by Labour prior to election to office that was not deferred by the balance of payments crisis of 1964/5. It is open to at least two interpretations. One, by those opposed to the reform, is that the Circular is uncompromising in its demand for reorganization. At the opposite extreme, the Circular is criticized for not setting out a uniform plan, and for the very fact that it is a Circular (a letter *requesting* action), rather than an Act of Parliament (making action compulsory). In many ways the Circular was a makeshift. It also reflected a concern, almost certainly embedded among Ministry officials, but probably shared by Labour politicians of the time, not to make too radical a break with the past; thus it was the aim 'to preserve all that is valuable in grammar school education for those children who now receive it and make it available to more children'. The drafters sailed between the Scylla of the opponents of reform and the Charybdis of its radical proponents. That the Circular succeeded in promoting reorganization by LEAs (if too quickly for the one, and too slowly for the other) is due to the Ministry's politic handling of the LEAs' obligation to submit plans. It is also a reflection of the extent to which the balance between local authority and central government was shifting in favour of the latter.

Far from establishing a clear-cut definition of comprehensive schooling, the Circular discussed the schemes that had already been adopted piecemeal by experimenting LEAs, and gave mild encouragement to some and gentle criticism to others.

These plans were of six types:

(i) All-through 11–18 schools;*
(ii) Two-tier schemes:
    (*a*) All pupils enter lower school at eleven and transfer to upper at thirteen or fourteen;*
    (*b*) All pupils enter lower school at eleven, but only some transfer to upper school; (interim)
    (*c*) All pupils enter lower school at eleven, and choose between two types of upper school at thirteen or fourteen, one for those expecting to stay well beyond the compulsory leaving age, the other for those not expecting to stay on; (interim)
(iii) Sixth form college: all pupils enter 11–16 school and transfer to the sixth form college if they wish to stay on; (?)
(iv) Middle school: all pupils transfer at eight or nine to a middle school, and then to a further comprehensive school at twelve or thirteen, with an age range to eighteen. (?)

The Ministry's attitude to each scheme is suggested by the asterisks – these were strongly recommended as long term solutions; by 'interim' – these were regarded as half way stages because they merely pushed selection back to thirteen or fourteen; and by the question mark – these were less proven, still experimental.

There were five themes in the Circular which reflect Ministerial caution about the change in policy and a somewhat naive understanding of the new venture. First, though it was 'selection' that was under attack, no attempt was made to *define* selection: since school systems of the 'interim' two-tier variety might depend upon examinations or teachers' reports for transfer at thirteen/fourteen, might leave future schooling to the choice of parent and child, or again might seek to *guide* that choice through teachers' advice, the term 'selection' covered a variety of practices. Clearly the 11–18 and automatic transfer two-tier systems appear to avoid such hazards of definition, but even they might be organized *internally* by 'selection' of some kind. The Circular did not even mention this problem, though it was already becoming well known in educational circles.

A second theme in the Circular was a preoccupation with fitting reorganization to existing buildings. Thus all-through schools would sometimes be too big for any one building that was available. On these grounds a two-tier scheme might be preferred and even a middle school scheme considered. One old Ministerial reservation about the all-through school – that it would become too big to manage if its intake was planned for a viable sixth form – was no longer at issue, since a far higher percentage was staying on into the sixth form. But it was still orthodoxy that one school should have one building.

The third element was reiteration of the old view that transfer from primary to secondary schooling should be at age eleven. However, the 1944 Act had been amended the previous year to make way for middle schools, and, within a year of the circular, without waiting for a Central Advisory Council Report on the matter, the Minister approved the middle school pattern to help ease reorganization in certain areas. Pragmatism prevailed over orthodoxy.

Fourthly, the circular urged local authorities to negotiate with voluntary aided schools in the hope of persuading them to join in comprehensive schemes, and to enter into discussions with direct grant schools with whom they took up places. An amending act of 1967 eased the way to the participation of voluntary aided schools. The participation of direct grant schools proved far more difficult to ensure. The Ministry either failed to anticipate this, or felt it unnecessary to include direct grant schools in comprehensive reorganization.

The fifth and final element was to require that local authority plans should be publicized and discussed with teachers involved and interested parents. The Ministry wished to devolve responsibility for the reform to LEAs rather than give them special powers. Most LEA schemes were compromises with sectional interests in the localities and designed to meet the constraints of existing buildings: as a result, especially in the large and thinly populated Counties, there was often a patchwork of schools with different age ranges and terms of entry. Unlike France, England did not build large numbers of new schools. Indeed the pitifully small capital allowance for new schools was taken up with alterations to old buildings. The Ministry under Labour blocked schemes that did not meet with government policy by wielding its sole tangible power over the LEAs – the right to refuse finance for a given building project. But this power was exercised in the relatively liberal spirit of the Circular.

Party politics and the local reforms after 1965

The progress of reorganization in the LEAs was closely correlated with the fluctuating fortunes of the two major parties in local government elections. These fluctuations are a striking feature of English politics in the 1960s and 1970s. For example, as was mentioned above, twenty County Boroughs had been in Labour control from 1945 to 1962; but by the end of the 1960s only six had stayed the course. As party positions on comprehensive reform hardened – they did so even more at local than at national level – which party controlled the Council became crucial to the speed with which plans were prepared, submitted to the Ministry and acted upon if approved. Many authorities changed party control and policy on reorganization at successive elections.

Counties are the exception that proves the rule. For (but for Lancashire) party control in the Counties remained relatively stable in the '60s and '70s. After 1967, Labour tended to lose control of the few Counties it had won in previous elections. The net effect was that while the Circular sped up the reorganization in the Counties, this reorganization was built upon earlier experiments in many cases and was not so sharply affected, positively or negatively, by government policy, as was reform in the urban areas. The survey of reorganization carried out by the Campaign for Comprehensive Education in 1972 (CCE, 1972) showed that two thirds of the twenty-five Counties who had pioneered comprehensive schools before 1962 had at least 25 per cent of the relevant age group in comprehensives by 1972, a position attained by only nine of the twenty-one Counties who had no comprehensives in 1962, for four of them had not begun comprehensive reorganization. Furthermore, only four of the forty-six Counties had 90 per cent or more of the age group in comprehensive schools by 1972, compared with 28 per cent of other authorities. Not one of the four had been in Labour control in this period.

The contrast with the County Boroughs and the London Boroughs may be seen in Tables 3.1 and 3.2.

Table 3.1 *County Boroughs: political control and comprehensivization*

Political control	Proportion of secondary age group in comprehensives 1972			
	90%+	25–89%	up to 25%	None
Labour through 1960s	3	2	—	1
Labour 1965 and 1966	16	10	7	9
Labour *lose* 1965 or 1966	1	1	3	6
Other control through 1960s	2	—	2	13

Sixty-five per cent of County Boroughs that were controlled by Labour at the crucial time had placed at least 25 per cent of the secondary age group in schools they called comprehensive by 1972. Only 14 per cent of the other LEAs had done so, and 68 per cent of them had made no progress at all.

London local government was reorganized in 1965. Twenty Outer London Boroughs were formed, one of them absorbing Middlesex. The London County Council (LCC) was discontinued. However, while each of the Outer Boroughs became an independent LEA, the Inner Boroughs were grouped for educational functions in the same geographical area as that governed by the LCC: this new authority was called the Inner London Education Authority (ILEA). In size alone this education authority is important. Its influence on the development of comprehensive schooling, both as LCC and ILEA is of greater significance still. The policy of setting up purpose-built comprehensives in war-damaged areas of the city began in the post-war period. But a large number of selective schools survived the war, and many were relatively autonomous, because of direct grant or 'voluntary aided' status. The authority compromised so that many of its comprehensive schools were heavily 'creamed' of high ability pupils. Setting this aside, ILEA inherited from LCC by far the longest list of schools called 'comprehensive' possessed by any LEA, while few of the Outer London Boroughs had even a single comprehensive passed on to them.

The politics of the London authorities founded in 1965 has been even more chequered than that of provincial authorities during the same period. Up to 1972 there were three elections for the Borough councils. In the first, Labour gained ten Outer Boroughs, plus ILEA, while the Conservatives, alone or in coalition, controlled the other ten. However, in 1968, the Conservatives gained a landslide victory, taking eighteen of the Outer Boroughs (all but Barking and Newham) *and* ILEA, an area which had not been in Conservative hands since before the War. In 1971, Labour recovered much of the ground it lost, and added two more boroughs to its tally of 1965: most significantly ILEA was once more in Labour control. Table 3.2 shows how far party control encouraged or impeded comprehensive reform to 1972.

Table 3.2 *London Boroughs: political control and comprehensivization*

| Political control | Proportion of secondary age group in comprehensives 1972 | | | |
	90%+	25–89%	up to 25%	None
Labour 1965–72	1	–	–	1
Labour 1965–67, lost 1968	4	1 plus ILEA	2	1
Gained Labour 1971	1	–	1	–
Other control	–	2	2	4

Though percentages sound unduly grandiose with such small numbers, it may be said that 64 per cent of LEAs in London that were controlled by Labour immediately after Circular 10/65 had placed at least 25 per cent of the age group in comprehensive schools by 1972, while 70 per cent of those out of Labour's hands in the crucial period had made little or no progress with the reform the Circular enjoined. These figures are comparable to those in the County Boroughs.

The electorate and local reorganization

In a few local authorities, the control of one party has been so consistent from election to election that the party group on Council has become a self-perpetuating oligarchy, which forms its policy in camera and imposes it, not only upon other interests, but upon other members of the same party. An example was Gateshead in the middle 1960s (Batley, O'Brien and Parris, 1970). In the great majority of Councils, especially during the 1960s and 1970s, party groups have expected a short term of office, and, as a result of their relatively precarious position, have had to negotiate policy with their rank and file and even with opposing interests. Darlington was an example of this more general pattern in the same period (idem).

In this concluding section of our discussion of the politics of the English comprehensive reform, we shall argue the tentative hypothesis that whichever party has controlled local Councils in the chequered period since 1965 has been obliged to turn an ear to 'the electorate'. In local as well as national elections, the predominant support of the Labour Party is working class, and it is in the most working class areas that Labour has held control most often. Even if the Conservative Party has taken temporary control in such an area, it has had difficulty in reversing Labour's policy. The converse applies to temporary Labour control of a predominantly middle class area. Thus social infrastructure not only makes probable the electoral victory of one party rather than another. It also constrains the policy of the party in power. By 'social infrastructure' is meant here the pattern of class relations within a locality and the direction in which it is changing. Ideally this involves knowing how people live, what groups they form, how such groups ally and conflict and whether in industry, the community or politics. For the most part, this information is lacking. Indirect measures from the Registrar General's Censuses and similar official sources offer some basis for comparing one local authority with another. One such measure may be called the 'index of working-classness'. It is based upon figures drawn from County Reports of the 1966 Sample Census, which was carried out in the midst of the period that particularly concerns us. Each area was ranked on seven dimensions, and assigned a score from one to four on each, depending upon whether it was in the top, second, third or fourth 25 per cent. Taking the seven dimensions together, an area could score 28 at one extreme and 7 at the other. The dimensions involved were the proportion of dwellings that (i) were owner occupied and (ii) were council houses; the proportion of households (iii) having their own hot water, bath and inside WC and (iv) with their own car; the proportion of economically active males who (v) were professionals and managers and (vi) were lower white collar workers and (vii) were unskilled manual workers. What such a measure so clearly lacks in 'flesh and blood', it may gain in stark impartiality.

We should expect the working-classness of an area to underpin its party preferences in local government. It is also possible that Labour may have gained control in areas that were less than

Table 3.3: *Social infrastructure, political control and comprehensivization*
(a) County Boroughs

| | Working-classness | | | |
| | 'High' 22–27 | | 'Low' 21 and lower | |
Political control	Comp. S 25%+	Under 25%	Comp. S 25%+	Under 25%
Labour 1965/66	19	10	12	7
Other control	3	4	1	20
	22	14	13	27

(b) London Boroughs

| | Working-classness | | | |
| | 'High' 11–26 | | 'Low' 10 and lower | |
Political control	Comp. S 25%+	Under 25%	Comp. S 25%+	Under 25%
Labour 1965/67	5 + ILEA	2	1	2
Other	2	—	1	7
	8	2	2	9

solidly working class with its popularity of 1965, or, more interesting, that whichever party was in power in a relatively working
class area, was under pressure to reorganize secondary education.
The pattern in the Boroughs of London and the provinces lends
support to all three of these expectations.

It will be readily seen that the Boroughs in London are less
likely to be working class than those outside. In fact only four
County Boroughs (Solihull, Southport, Southend and Bourne-
mouth) are as low on the index as those eleven that are called
'Low' in London. Yet the relative positions of London Boroughs
on the index are no less related to how far they had gone comprehensive by 1972, than are those of the County Boroughs to
their degree of comprehensivization. Sixty-one per of County
Boroughs that were 'High' on this scale had 25 per cent or more
of the secondary age group in comprehensives in 1972; while 68
per cent that were 'Low' had fewer than 25 per cent reorganized.
As for the London LEAs, if we include ILEA, 80 per cent of those
that were relatively high in working-classness had 50 per cent or
more in comprehensives by 1972, but 82 per cent of those that
were low had under 25 per cent.

In both contexts, the class composition of the area, which party
controls, and the degree of comprehensivization achieved by the
LEA seem to match in the majority of cases: for thirty-nine out
of seventy-six County Boroughs and thirteen out of twenty-one
London LEAs. Within London, Labour pushed through comprehensivization in only one Borough with a 'low' score on the
working-classness index, that is Enfield. On the other hand, social
infrastructure seemed to prevail against party politics in four
authorities – Merton and Croydon, a little higher on the index
than most that were Conservative controlled in 1965/7, were
well ahead with reorganization by 1972; while Bexley and Hil-
lingdon, much lower in working-classness than other boroughs
that Labour gained in the election of 1965, may have been too
intractable for reorganization. By contrast, in the County
Boroughs, party control seems to have been marginally more
often decisive than working-classness for the reform. There were
sixteen cases – four areas that were heavily working class, yet not
controlled by Labour which made little progress with the reform
and twelve that were lower on the index, but controlled by

Labour and well ahead by 1972. Social infrastructure appeared to overcome the party in power in ten cases, ranging from Birmingham, Conservative controlled yet relatively working class and with 28 per cent in comprehensives, to Southport, which was controlled by a Liberal/Labour coalition in 1965 and 1966 that could make less headway with a reform of education.

Only fourteen cases (three in London) defy explanation either by which party was in control at the crucial time or by social infrastructure making reform less resistable or more intractable. Only two of these were Conservative controlled boroughs, middle class in composition, which had progressed far towards reorganization by 1972 (Barnet in London, and Wallasey in Cheshire). The rest were all working class, Labour controlled in 1965/7 and yet little advanced if at all on the path to reorganization by 1972. Undoubtedly there are many local contingencies that might explain these 'deviant cases', and it must be pointed out that all but three of these authorities had started belatedly on their reforms by the time local government reorganization obliterated most of them in 1974. On the other hand, many of them may be said to contain large working class housing areas that have remained relatively unchanged for up to a hundred years: Hartlepool, Bootle, Salford, Barnsley, Dewsbury, Liverpool, Warrington, South Shields, Barrow, Great Yarmouth and Newham (London). Of the ten County Boroughs on this list nine are in the top 35 (out of 79) on the index score for working-classness; and six are in the top thirteen. By the same token, Newham is far and away the most working class borough in London.

What significance can be attached to this flickering picture of the relation between infrastructure, party control and the implementation of comprehensive reform in LEAs?

There can be no doubt that comprehensive reform was a burning issue in local politics. The problem is what set it alight, and what kept it burning. It was not simply the Labour government's alteration of long-standing Ministry policy in favour of selective schooling, for there was increasingly urgent debate of the issue and planning for reform from the late 1950s. We would suggest that education officers and local Labour Party groups alike were responding to pressures originating in the new middle classes and felt within the tripartite system. This is reflected in education officers' early efforts to modify and even to abandon selection at 11-plus. It is also indicated by the shift of emphasis in discussions of the comprehensive school from egalitarianism to efficiency. The pressures did not come to a head until the late 1950s. Labour's post-1959 electoral policy gave expression to new middle class sentiments.

This is what set the issue alight. Whether this kept it burning after Labour's accession to office in 1964 is another matter. It is of considerable interest that, in spite of Labour's appeal to the centre, and the similar policy adopted by Mr Heath in opposition, there was enough controversy at local level to promote far greater fluctuations in party control of the local authorities than had been seen since the war. One of the most prominent elements in the controversy was comprehensive schooling. So lively a debate must have been fuelled by clashes of interest among sections of the electorate. The difficulty any party group had in maintaining control of the Council from election to election, meant that it must respond to these interests, and in particular to the one that dominated in its locality. The pattern of advance of comprehensive reform from authority to authority suggests that there was an alignment, roughly speaking, of working class against middle class. Where either predominated, a party which contradicted its interests would have difficulty maintaining the party line on comprehensive reform.

It seems that for a time the reorganization of secondary schooling was lost to the new middle classes who (inadvertently in most cases) set it in motion, and was captured by the working class. The working class interest in reform is unlikely to be the social advancement of their children. In the early 1960s the Labour Party believed that prosperity had weaned many workers from their traditional attachment to Labour, and that their social outlook now resembled that of the middle class. A critical test of this 'embourgeoisement' thesis among affluent workers in the growth town of Luton during the middle 1960s, showed that these workers were probably more home-centred than the 'traditional' working class of the older urban-industrial areas, and more 'instrumental' in their attitude to their jobs and the union; but they had not changed their party allegiance, and they did not share the passion for social advancement of the middle classes (Goldthorpe *et al.*, 1969). Furthermore, unlike the traditional workers, most affluent workers felt there was no impermeable barrier between the middle and working classes, but instead differences of income, and thus purchasing power, of doubtful legitimacy. This radical and optimistic egalitarianism may have inspired working class interest in comprehensivization in localities where the older housing patterns and means of employment were breaking down. If so it was an 'education-consciousness' different from that of the middle class – even opposed to it. In areas where the traditional working class predominated, not only would there have been a lack of interest in education for the advancement of one's children, but also a sense that the inequalities of society were too embedded to admit reform by schooling.

Whether egalitarian aims can be met by comprehensive schools is a question we must address in what follows. It must be said immediately that whatever influence workers or other parents might have had on the *foundation* of comprehensive schools, it was teachers who ran them and developed their organization and curricula. It is time to enter the schools themselves.

4

The organization of comprehensive schools

Size

It has often been said that, whatever the educational and social merits of comprehensive schools, they are too big: they make the individual pupil (and teacher) feel anonymous, and may, as a result, breed disorder; further, they are unwieldy to manage.

'Too big' is a relative term. In the days of early experiments with comprehensive schooling in England, it meant around 2000 pupils, which was a size not uncommon among urban high schools in the United States and chosen for several English schools especially in London, Bristol and Coventry. In the last ten years the typical size of English comprehensive schools has shrunk. To an extent this is because more pupils are staying on and being admitted to the sixth form. An early argument for large comprehensive schools in England was that only ten to twelve form entry could command an adequate sixth form. Now a school of around 1000 pupils or six/seven form entry is 'big enough' on this criterion. On the other hand, like the 2000-pupil school of twenty years ago, the 1000-pupil school of today is sometimes said to be 'too big' for the individual and too big to manage.

The best size for an organization has been a subject of much speculation among workers, administrators and academic theorists in business and public service contexts. On the face of it, size is more readily experienced and measured than all other features of organizations. If you cannot fix the best *size* for an organization, how can you decide what is the best way of communicating within it or what best develops morale among workers? Perhaps size is in any case the key to all these other less tangible problems.

The most relevant study of size of school as a factor in morale and learning among pupils was carried out in the United States some years ago (Barker and Gump, 1964). Its findings – like so many in educational research – give little comfort to either side: either to those who believe big schools lead to low morale or to those who argue that big schools give a wider choice of subjects to their pupils. It was found that for pupils, the psychologically significant work setting was the class with whom they met most often, and that this was a more direct influence upon them than the size of the school. At the same time it did not necessarily follow that the larger schools gave each pupil a wider education than he could gain in a smaller school. The number of subjects offered was usually greater in the large school, but for timetabling reasons the breadth of choice open to individuals was no greater than in the smaller schools. The authors tend to favour small schools in their conclusion, but this seems to be more because they can see no good reason to sweep them away, as was the trend at the time in USA, than because there are decisive advantages to be found in the smaller organization.

In England there is considerable prejudice in favour of smaller schools. Thus, as the increased rate of staying on into the sixth form has permitted it, the norm for a comprehensive school – an all-through school that is – has been reduced. This has also been a factor in favour of two-tier and middle school patterns of secondary school reorganization. What may lie behind this is the strong institutional position of the English head teacher. Compared with his counterpart in USA, France or Sweden he has considerable autonomy for designing the curriculum, for setting disciplinary policy and for dictating managerial organization within the school. It is expected that a head *will lead* rather than delegate his powers. Further, he is supposed to manage the school through knowing teachers and pupils personally, rather than by formal and impersonal methods, such as regulations and memoranda. Many heads believe they should teach as well as administer. Such paternalism is more readily exercised in a small than a large organization. Heads and teachers, too, are more at home with paternalism than 'administration'.

The growing fashion for heads to see themselves as 'administrators' and for sending heads on formal courses in universities and colleges of education which teach 'educational administration' resembles a development after the war in the United States. It parallels the shift to schools that are larger and cannot readily be managed by one man's knowledge of his staff and pupils. However, whereas in the United States 'administration' is associated with business and its prestige, in England it tends to be seen as an excrescence which chokes good practice – as 'bureaucracy' in the everyday sense. Thus educational administration and the larger schools that go with it have an up-hill struggle to establish themselves with teachers and probably also with academics.

However, the fundamental basis of resistance to the large school may lie at a more mundane level than ideas and attitudes. Formal organizations and their physical plant are like virgin land: what gives each its social and psychological character is the way that people have *colonized* it. In other words, it is the multifarious identities and social relations that people form in playing the prescribed roles of teacher, head and pupil in a building with its equipment that makes 'a school', rather than resources or terms of appointment and admission, though these are limits on the practices that people can develop. Colonization takes time. A teacher who had been in a purpose-built comprehensive over the thirteen years since it was founded described the school in its early days as a 'concentration camp', while another in a similar school said that at first teachers and pupils felt they rattled in the buildings like dry peas in a pod. After some years of colonization the sense of so hostile an environment disappeared in both schools.

The reorganization of existing schools to form comprehensives also puts teachers into something of a hostile environment. It may compound this effect by tearing down well-founded identities and relations and requiring a renegotiation of both in the face of new colleagues and a new head, as well as new pupils. Top management castigates employees who resist new working conditions – 'resistance to change' is a common topic for research in industry by sociologists and psychologists – and 'adaptability' is the aim of much occupational training, even of general education. What is sometimes overlooked is that not only 'attitudes' have to be changed to match new conditions but also relations of power, prestige and friendship built up in daily work over time. These are no more irrelevant to the running of an organization than is administration. They help to explain why comprehensive schools are seen as 'too big' by their staff. For teachers who have come from smaller schools may look back on the identities and relations they have lost with rose-tinted spectacles, because they find it hard to rearrange their lives in the new setting.

Problems of management in secondary schools

That the new comprehensive schools are 'too big' is perhaps an illusion with a basis in the reality of teachers' disrupted social relations with each other and with pupils. There are, of course, *real* problems of management in comprehensive schools. Many, however, are shared with English secondary schools generally.

These perennial problems exist at two levels – the class teacher's management of his lessons and the co-ordination of various class teachers' activities. Obviously the need for co-ordination increases as the division of labour between specialist teachers becomes more advanced. Schools, like many smaller primaries, in which pupils are grouped only by age and each class has one teacher for all subjects, have little division of labour. In secondary schools, remedial classes apart, pupils are usually differentiated *within* the year group and each of their subjects may be taught by a separate teacher. This relatively advanced division of labour not only calls for co-ordination between teachers, it also affects the individual teacher's management of his lessons, since contact time with any one group of pupils is limited and fragmentary.

77

Within each lesson the individual secondary teacher has to match a programme of learning to the aptitudes of his pupils, to motivate them and to make the exercise satisfactory by his own standards. Motivating pupils is perhaps the most complex task. It involves cutting out distractions and finding something to stimulate the pupils' interests. Since each pupil is one of a class of around thirty others, the teacher must manipulate social processes within the class if he is to motivate any one pupil. What is more, each teacher's way of solving the problems of motivation becomes a problem in turn to his colleagues who teach the class. They have to copy his approach or counteract it.

Co-ordinating the activities of different teachers is only partly an exercise of administration. The prime administrative instrument is the timetable, by means of which different teachers are allocated to various classes in sequence. The overall balance of courses, the content of each course and the supply of equipment for lessons will normally be decided by the head and his deputies and in departmental meetings. Beyond these rudimentary bases of co-ordination, such interlinks as there are between individual teachers are maintained by persuasion from above and by colleagues and pupils.

One head of a comprehensive school known to the author took the view that consistency in discipline both outside and within lessons was important not only for order but also for motivation and learning (Bellaby, 1975). He provided each teacher with a manual outlining school rules and permitted forms of punishment for breaking them, together with advice about how to cope with new classes. Another tried to influence the style of control his teachers exercised in lessons by insisting that each award at least ten 'positive' points and no more than two 'negative' points per week, while no one should detain individual pupils on their own initiative, since pupils could only be sentenced to detention after school hours if they had accumulated two negative points in a week without sufficient compensation in positive points. Many teachers obeyed this in the letter more than the spirit, especially with fourth and higher year pupils. Nevertheless the head attempted openly to produce a common front on control in lessons. Another head may have been more typical in that his attitudes on discipline were well known (and widely practised) by his staff, though the only example he set out to give was in control of morning assembly and of passage up and down the corridors.

However, teachers also influence each other and are influenced by the pupils they teach in this respect. New teachers tend to be guided by the more experienced and prestigious in the school, whatever the disparity between their training and the practices they encounter there. Weak disciplinarians and teachers with ideas out of line with the dominant group in the staff room are known as such, and though they may only be mentioned behind their backs, discover by non-verbal cues what attitude others take to them. Since pupils form expectations of what teachers will do when starting and closing lessons, in the event of a disturbance and so on, and what they will wear and how they will speak, they too force a measure of conformity upon individual teachers. Their awareness of the typical approach of their teachers and how anxious the unfamiliar teacher tends to be to keep in line, is often illustrated by the games they play with students on teaching practice. They want to trap the student into a too permissive or too harsh style of control, or to make him slip up as he reads his lines. With a new permanent teacher pupils are inclined to be cautious, but they and the teacher will be aware of the need to strike some bargain from an early stage within the going terms dictated by habitual practice among teachers and their classes.

Thus a great deal of the co-ordination which is achieved between teachers in a secondary school is not by formal rules, but rather informal social processes. It is obvious that such processes are a product of what we have called 'colonization' and therefore need time and a fairly settled population to emerge. Co-ordination, especially in matters of discipline and motivation of pupils, may be hard to achieve in a new or reorganized school by any means short of concerted repression of pupils. The school the teacher we quoted called a 'concentration camp' in its earlier days, adopted this kind of policy. It was made possible by the fact that many members of staff stayed with the head, that there was a more than proportionate number of middle class boys and girls in its intake and that the school quickly made its mark academically in competition with others in the same town. Most schools, like another in the town, which was more working class, less 'successful' and had higher staff turnover, might have a time of troubles both in discipline and in staff management, before staff established a co-ordinated approach to lessons.

In the early period, heads may be credited with heroic status or seen as total failures by the extent to which they match up to their institutionalized position and take a 'firm lead'. This lead must be of a rather specific content. In particular, the head should stand up for teachers in the face of challenge by parents or their children. The need to protect 'authority' by closing the ranks is proportionate to how insecure that authority is. Plainly teachers will feel more strongly about being 'let down' by the head when a recalcitrant pupil is sent for the cane or a dressing down in the early stages of a school than when a co-ordinated policy has emerged. The reaction of many teachers to Duane's insistence at Risinghill Comprehensive on *not* punishing tough cases, illustrates the thesis (Berg, 1968). As a result of their reaction, Duane was branded as a failure and his school closed by the local authority. By striking contrast, the head of what once resembled a 'concentration camp' was regarded as a hero by his staff and eventually appeared in the Queen's Honours List. This particular head's demeanour and dress in school and the calm control he exercised over assemblies and the corridor near his office contributed to the respect he earned from most of his staff. It is important, however, to note that a head's performance is *socially* produced and constrained. Just as Homer's heroes fought their way through obstacles put there by the gods to achieve a destiny the gods ordained, so successful heads become so on terms their teachers lay down.

'Mix a grammar school and a secondary modern . . .'

Putting staff into a comprehensive school does not automatically change their approach to teaching. Three mixed 11–18 schools in the same town this author has studied combined in varying degrees young teachers fresh to comprehensives, teachers with previous experience in secondary moderns and those who had taught in grammar or technical schools (Bellaby, 1975). One had been viewed by the public in the town as their 'grammar school' before becoming a full comprehensive in 1962, and the majority of its staff had the typical background of grammar school teachers

80

– they were graduates of a university. We may call it 'Castle Town'. In another school in the same town, 'Hinsley Mill', the bias had been towards technical education and a majority of teachers held certificates from training colleges rather than university degrees. Both these schools had a lower turnover of staff and older teachers on average than the third school, 'Cross Street', which was in the most working class area of the town. Castle Town had won a series of open awards at Oxford and Cambridge colleges, and Hinsley Mill (in spite of its supposedly 'technical' stream of selective pupils) had a performance at what in the 1950s and early 1960s was the pinnacle of grammar school ambitions, not far short of Castle Town's. Cross Street was the Cinderella of the three schools. Though, like Hinsley Mill, it began with a technical selective stream, its reputation was that of a struggling secondary modern school. Its staff was weighted rather heavily towards those taking up their first jobs, usually fresh from training college.

Castle Town's head came from a famous northern grammar school. His task and that of most of his staff was to translate the grammar school tradition into a context where pupils of all abilities were to be taught. The seven form entry who had reached the third year in 1966/7 were streamed from the beginning, and the top two streams had an almost unrelievedly academic curriculum and were expected to enter for O-level GCE, the first at the end of the fourth year (an 'express-stream'), and the second at the end of the fifth. At the same time the staff of this school was acutely aware that pupils in lower streams should receive the attention of the most experienced teachers, though the bottom three streams were not likely to be entered for more than the odd CSE even if they stayed until the end of the fifth year. Graduates and heads of department were as likely to teach lower as upper streams.

Hinsley Mill school grew under the shadow of Castle Town. The translation of the grammar school tradition into Hinsley Mill was different in several respects to its adaptation in Castle Town. Hinsley Mill had no express stream, and it taught the top two streams handicraft in place of Latin. More important, rather than keeping the streams much as they had been since the children entered the school, Hinsley Mill made streaming into a sort of League Table in which exceptional achievement was rewarded by promotion and failure by demotion. Promotions and demotions were sometimes made at termly intervals, and the same pupil could go up and down a number of times. Hinsley Mill's streaming policy resembled what Young has called 'achievement streaming', while Castle Town's policy was closer to his 'ability streaming' (Young, 1967). Not least among the rewards of achievement at Hinsley Mill was that you might gain the chance of being taught by a graduate, a more experienced teacher or a head of department. The staff were distributed unevenly between the streams, and the lower tended to receive part-time women teachers, who were absent rather more frequently and less in touch with school policy than others.

The third school, Cross Street, was in 1966/7 balanced between the strategy adopted with far more success by Hinsley Mill and 'going progressive'. Its current third year had been streamed since entry and promoted and demoted between streams as frequently as Hinsley Mill's. However, this was the school mentioned earlier whose head had introduced a system of 'points' designed to bias class teachers in favour of reward and away from punishment. In addition each form had a tutor with special responsibility for the welfare of its members, who met it regularly throughout the week. In that same year, the school was beginning mixed ability teaching during the first year.

There can be little doubt that the school's working class (and 'secondary modern') image helped to push it in this direction. Staff frequently complained that by comparison with Hinsley Mill they had few pupils of selective ability, or that they had a working class rather than a middle class intake. This was not strictly correct, since Hinsley Mill was also predominantly working class. The order of difference between the schools was that Hinsley Mill was two fifths middle class in intake, and Cross Street about a quarter, if 'middle class' is taken to be non-manual workers and those in supervisory positions. However, the image that teachers had of the two schools was what shaped their approach to teaching not the 'facts' of their class-composition. This image was a form of rationalization for the less good academic record of Cross Street school. It also contributed to staff leaving after between two and three years on average rather than four as at the other two schools, and to the fact that a high proportion of Cross Street teachers were new to teaching. It seems that schools with good reputations find it easy to enhance them by attracting the best staff. Perhaps those who do not succeed academically must find alternative criteria of excellence. Two or three years ago Cross Street was advertising nationally for a head of department post, and the advertisement made the main attraction of the school its 'progressive' policies of non-streaming and tutorial groups.

Discipline and the comprehensive school

The reorganization of secondary education in England has been accompanied by a deepening controversy about discipline in schools, and a feeling on the part of many teachers, especially members of the National Association of Schoolmasters, that schools are becoming more disordered and in some cases violent. It is widely assumed that England has become more 'permissive', or less 'authoritarian', depending upon whether the 'fact' is deplored or welcomed. Schools are supposed to reflect this trend.

The problems adolescence in general and the unmotivated pupil in particular pose for teachers are common to all secondary schools. Clearly they are concentrated in the secondary modern schools, and in the lower streams of these and grammar schools alike (Hargreaves, 1967; Lacey, 1970). Putting adolescents under a similar type of schooling merely within a common building is unlikely to have an effect on the pattern for good or ill. But, as we have already discovered, teachers' definitions of the comprehensive school in which they work, influence their approach to school organization and teaching. Further, there are some shifts in the philosophy of the 'good comprehensive' which must have implications for discipline and order in these schools.

The author's study of Castle Town, Hinsley Mill and Cross Street schools throws some light on these questions. To summarize what has been reported about them: in Castle Town, the grammar school tradition was adapted to a comprehensive setting by staff with grammar-type background and qualifications. In Hinsley Mill the grammar school tradition was emulated, but by teachers with technical and secondary modern backgrounds. As a result, while Castle Town adopted 'ability' streaming, Hinsley Mill used 'achievement' streaming. Cross Street was wavering between a strategy like Hinsley Mill's, which it had pursued with less obvious success, and making its name as a 'progressive' institution. Its staff was young and relatively inexperienced, and they believed that their school had less than its share of high ability pupils.

So far as discipline was concerned, Hinsley Mill put far more pressure on its pupils to succeed academically and conduct themselves according to school protocol than did Castle Town. Castle Town was an easy-going regime. The stringency of Hinsley Mill accorded with the style of streaming in that school. However, permissiveness is by no means invariable among teachers used to grammar school teaching. At Castle Town it seemed to be an adaptation to the wider ability range, and for some teachers to mixed classes of boys and girls. *Their* problem was to teach the 'secondary modern' pupils, whereas the problem for Hinsley Mill teachers was to make the most of the selective streams. So far as the Castle Town teachers were concerned the upper streams responded of their own free will, needing little pressure, and those lower down co-operated if they were not made to jump through hoops that did not fit them. This is not to say that the lower streams were neglected. On the contrary, as we have seen, they received their full share of attention from the most qualified and experienced teachers. However, some teachers at Castle Town felt that they were doing a disservice to their pupils by their relatively relaxed and informal style of teaching.

The Hinsley Mill staff were, with few exceptions, fully committed to an 'autarchic' form of teaching, in which the teacher fed most of the material to the class, dictated pupils' conduct and was somewhat critical or censorious about their academic performance. They derived satisfaction from the sense that 'work was being done' in all their classes, even if in fact, with lower streams, this frequently amounted to no more than the classes copying a map or diagram from the board and colouring it.

Neither Hinsley Mill nor Castle Town seemed to have serious problems of disorder. However, Hinsley Mill used detentions after school about three times as often as the other school. In lessons observed by the author with upper and lower third year classes, teachers at Hinsley Mill were the more directive and gave more rebukes per hour than their counterparts in the town's old 'grammar school'. This pattern was remarkably consistent from teacher to teacher in the two schools.

When third year pupils were asked to report their own conduct at school and their feelings about various aspects of discipline and teachers' use of authority, the Hinsley Mill boys and girls proved more hostile to staff than those at Castle Town. This hostility seldom showed in classes, though there was the odd boy or girl who had gained a lurid reputation for expressing what many others felt: like the boy who sent an order of surgical appliances to his form teacher's address, or the girl who stormed out of class accusing her teacher of victimization. There was no counterpart to this at Castle Town. Indeed, within the third year there was no single form which was a clear cut example of an 'anti-school' culture. At Hinsley Mill, three of the six streams showed signs of being united (at least covertly) in opposition to teachers, among other things by making the most daring misbehavers their most popular peers. However, by the standards of many Castle Town teachers, quite apart from those at Hinsley Mill, and in the estimation of the Education Officer, Castle Town was an ill-managed and disorderly school, in sharp distinction to Hinsley Mill.

Cross Street was praised by the Education Officer for trying to build a clear framework within which its pupils could find themselves and become committed to school work. The framework she had in mind was the system of tutorial groups and the use of positive points as a spur to conduct and achievement. These were inspired by the head. The specific design of the system was due to a committee of teachers, and of course it was individual teachers who implemented it. The operation of the system did not accord entirely with the head's objectives. First, much like the teachers at Hinsley Mill, those at Cross Street tried to use the 'selective' or top streams to the full. Heads of department and graduates taught these rather than lower streams. They adopted a censorious attitude to them both in and out of class. Secondly, they punished the lower streams far more often than the positive points arrangement allowed. The earliest breach of this was that the teachers' committee introduced *negative* points, and a competition between forms for the award of a points trophy. Lower streams tended to collect a disproportionate number of negative points. Since negative points counted against the form's tally of positives in the ratio 2:1, it was common to find higher streams winning the trophy while the lower streams' reputation with teachers and other pupils for being the roughs was reinforced by weekly announcement of the results of the competition. Thirdly, the success of the tutorial group depended greatly on the individual teacher. The tutorial group was not a mixture of different streams or age groups as is sometimes the case, but one and the same group in which children were taught. The tutor was expected to stay with the group until it was broken up in the fourth year, and to teach it. This was in addition to meeting with the group every morning and afternoon for registration and every other day and last thing in the week for a longer period, during which communal extra-curricular activities and pastoral work was called on. Of the two forms the author observed intimately, one had a tutor who was extremely conscientious, while the other paid no particular attention to the aims of the tutorial arrangement and allowed tutorial periods to be used for private homework. The group with the good tutor was a lower stream. Even so, the tutor was the only teacher who had full and unstrained control of the group. His influence did not extend to the class's conduct with other members of staff, though he tried hard to persuade teachers who claimed that his class was exceptionally difficult, that the pupils would respond to his kind of firm but patently interested and concerned attention.

Cross Street did provide a framework for its pupils, but not the system of rewards and pastoral care it appeared to be at first sight. The pupils were less uncertain in their ideas of what teachers expected of them than their counterparts in Hinsley Mill and Castle Town. However, a high proportion, especially in middle and lower streams, saw teachers as directive and punitive. If they were not so often extremely hostile to staff as were many at Hinsley Mill, they were less orderly in class and in moving around the school from lesson to lesson. The experience of disorder, especially in middle and lower streams, reinforced the tendency of teachers to rebuke and punish. What was missing at Cross Street, though present at Hinsley Mill, was a co-ordinated front on discipline – a team performance, led by the head teacher. Consequently teachers' individual attempts to impose order on classes would rebound upon them or upon the class teacher who followed them into the room. They actually *created* disorder.

A consistent feature of the response of pupils to the approach of teachers in the three schools was that those who looked forward to staying at school to take O-levels or CSEs in order to set themselves on the road to professional, managerial or technical careers, tended to accept authority and by and large to obey in class, while those who expected to leave at the earliest opportunity having made up their minds that a lower status job requiring less formal education was their lot, were more likely to reject authority and be disobedient. For the former, the 'Ambitious', schooling was a bridge to adult status, while for the latter, the 'Leavers', it was an obstacle to their getting a job or starting out towards marriage.

The 'grammar school tradition' has been plainly associated with the Ambitious. For them success at school is a game with its distinctive rules, which you learn by watching the teachers. The game is markedly different from 'playing' or teenage leisure pursuits, and consists, Keddie's research suggests, of knowing what questions to ask and answers to give when an issue is being discussed academically rather than in terms of everyday life (Keddie, 1971). Achievement streaming, as at Hinsley Mill, is a way of spurring on pupils who are thought unlikely to know how to play the game in advance, so that they quickly assimilate the rules. It consists of increasing the tension between the classroom and the pupils' world outside. The teachers at Castle Town did not see the Ambitious pupils' conduct as a particular problem. Such pupils knew the game already. There was nothing to be gained by trying to teach it to lower streams. Thus Castle Town relaxed the tension that many of its teachers had experienced in their own schooling and as teachers at grammar school.

Cross Street was torn between emulating Hinsley Mill, which it attempted unsuccessfully, and turning 'progressive'. These were contradictory aims. Progressivism presents an alternative theory to the grammar school tradition: instead of starting with the classics (including standard examples in physics as well as Latin and Greek or the great works of literature), the teacher builds on the interests of the pupils and encourages them to learn by discovering for themselves. Thus rather than heightening the tension between schooling and the pupils' world outside, progressivism seeks to bridge the gap by inducing children to learn principles from the things they are already familiar with. Cross Street's progressivism was more superficial and formal than this.

The study of the three schools shows how, at an early stage in the secondary school reorganization of the last decade, the grammar school tradition was very much alive within newly constituted comprehensive schools. Further the subsequent trend towards progressivism may have sprung from the same source, for many schools must have found, like Cross Street, that the grammar school tradition could not be forced upon working class pupils without causing disappointment and disorder.

The impact of trends in school organization on pupils' attitudes and conduct

We can only speculate about where secondary school reorganization is taking us, as mixed ability teaching becomes more widespread and a reform of that hitherto dominant legacy of the grammar school tradition, the GCE, is pending. We can find in a study of a California high school, a possible indication of the response of pupils to present day trends in English schools (Stinchcombe, 1964; Bellaby, 1974)

Stinchcombe's school was relatively academic. Sport and informal grouping among the pupils ('crowds') were of less significance there than in several high schools studied by earlier writers. Since sport plays a subordinate role in English schools, and the school is not normally a focus of teenage leisure life, Stinchcombe's high school is more like ours than many in the United States.

In this school pupils were not formally differentiated until the ninth grade (on the verge of senior or upper secondary education, as is now the pattern in Sweden; our equivalent in age, because of earlier starting, would be thirteen/fourteen years). At this stage they opted for one of several 'tracks', one general or academic, another technical (manual skills) and another commercial. In pupils' and parents' eyes the track to be preferred was the academic, since through it one could enter college (higher education) at graduation from high school. However, through past performance with teachers' guidance many parents and pupils had come to the conclusion that the academic track was simply inaccessible. These tended to be working class boys and girls. Because they were under less pressure to succeed than boys, working class girls in the non-academic track reconciled themselves to the implications for their future; many of them looked to nothing more than marriage. Some working class boys, but more so those middle class boys who found themselves forced by realities into a different track than the academic, could not reconcile themselves to the fact. They had been taught in home and at school that all had an equal chance to succeed, and the best won through. The penalty of falling behind in open contest is a sense of failure. Their short-run adaptation was to rebel from school – as it were, to *say* that school was unimportant while *feeling* injured by the unfavourable judgement it had passed on them. In neo-Freudian terms this constitutes a 'reaction-formation'. Its outward manifestation in this case was truancy, joy riding in cars, misbehaviour in class.

The pattern the author found in the three English comprehensives was different. The pupils who were hostile to school were overwhelmingly working class and included girls. They rejected not the fact that they were in low streams, but 'oppression' – being pushed around or made to do work and conduct themselves in ways for which they could see no pay-off or justification. At one level, the basis of the difference lies in the presence of formal academic differentiation at an early stage in English schools and its absence in the United States. The bulk of the English children probably were reconciled, even before they entered the comprehensive school, to what was likely to be their future status. Streaming in the comprehensive school was the main basis on which aspirations for the future were formed, rather than class background, but since there were relatively few middle class children in lower streams or working class children in upper streams, background and stream usually reinforced each other. Many American children, especially the working class girls were prepared as well, but the margin of uncertainty, most of all for middle class boys, was greater in the United States than England. At a deeper level we were witnessing in England, even within

89

comprehensive schools, the logic of sponsored mobility, of picking out children early on and preparing the most promising for elite status, the rest being seen as 'proles' in Orwell's sense. In the United States we find precisely the same sorting out, but without the formal intervention of teachers and education authorities, rather by open contest, at least for those who did not count themselves out to begin with by sex, class or race. The effect of such a contest is to shift the main penalties of schooling to those who 'fail' from those to whom it is irrelevant.

5

The outcomes of comprehensive schooling: a sociological appraisal

Three kinds of claim are made for comprehensive schooling: educational, egalitarian or social, and communitarian – though they are not always separated and are not necessarily opposed to each other.

The educational argument amounts to saying that comprehensive schools can develop talent better than selective schools. It is a worthy aim to make the most of everyone's varied abilities for *their* sake. But when the term 'talent' is used in this debate, it usually means *academic potential*. It is commonly assumed that society needs this type of gift more than most, and that schooling can develop it and ensure that those who have it are put in the highest positions in the professions, in industry and in government. As we have seen, this 'technical-function' theory takes for granted the capitalist relations of production that sustain it, and it is probably a mistaken view of the relation between school and economy. In treating the educational argument for comprehensive schooling, we shall ignore the problematic assumptions about school and economy, and deal only with the relative capacities of

91

comprehensive and selective systems to identify and develop academic potential.

The egalitarian argument forces us to examine further the links between school and *social structure*. For it is founded on the belief that selective schools reinforce existing disparities between social classes, or even create them, and that, by delaying selection, comprehensive schools can improve the opportunities of those born into disadvantaged families.

Finally, the communitarian argument is that, by serving a neighbourhood, the comprehensive school can diminish tensions, remove hostile stereotypes and cement solidarity, thus providing a focus for the enrichment of everyone's life, adults as well as children.

The educational argument

(i) *Waste and early selection in the tripartite system and comprehensive schools*

In an influential book, Ford has suggested that comprehensive schools do not necessarily do away with early selection (Ford, 1969). They merely transfer differentiation from the LEAs' 11-plus examination to their own streaming practices. She implies by her interpretation of a comparative study of a comprehensive, a grammar school and a modern school, that the streamed comprehensive school has similar effects to the tripartite system, and thus, among other things, cannot develop talent any further than grammar and modern schools. An earlier study by Holly seems to support this view, though he examined only the effect of streaming within a comprehensive school, and did not compare that school with grammar and modern schools (Holly, 1965). The academic differentiation which, according to the Benn and Simon surveys, most comprehensive schools practice, if to a diminishing extent, is thus characterized as defeating the educational objectives of the reform (Benn and Simon, 1972).

However, there are two assumptions here that need careful examination. The first is that early selection *does* impede the development of talent, and the second that any flaws there may be in selection for *different schools* remain when children are streamed within a comprehensive school.

Early selection is often justified precisely on the grounds that it develops talent to the full. The idea is that children must be identified and given specialist and intensive training from a relatively early age if their abilities are not to be wasted. This view is put into practice in music education in the USSR and Japan; the USSR and some cities in the USA also select promising mathematicians and others with what appear early on to be exceptional academic gifts and send them to special schools. There is, of course, more than a difference of degree between applying this argument to the education of the very few children with specific gifts, and applying it to the selection of 20 per cent or more who are above average general ability. USSR, USA and Japan today virtually take for granted the comprehensive organization of primary and secondary schooling for all but a tiny minority of the most gifted (and the most disadvantaged). The early selection of a relatively broad band of above average general ability is probably more subject to error, and, if segregation of children of different abilities for different schooling *is* socially divisive, worse in this respect too. But, however valid this observation, it does not follow that those of relatively high ability can look after themselves rather than requiring attention geared to their interests and abilities. Nor that they might not be 'held back' by pursuing the same curriculum at the same pace as less able children.

The view that early selection *impedes* the development of talent is directed less at those of relatively high ability than at those whose ability cannot be identified early and emerges later – the so-called 'late developers'. It is also reinforced by the belief that early selection is, at least in part, a 'self-fulfilling prophecy'. This means that children who are picked out as better, are lifted by the fact and make an improvement, which will be sustained by future success. On the other hand, those who are rejected will lose heart and repeated failure will depress their performance consistently. Rosenthal's experiment with deceiving teachers that some pupils in their classes had high marks in tests of general ability and attainment is often cited in support of this belief (Rosenthal and Jacobson, 1968). The pupils were given false scores and the 'best' scores reported to the teachers. After a period of months the experimenters tested all the children again to discover that those with the imputed high scores had made more progress than other children. The conclusion was that teachers' expectations of these pupils had been manifested in encouragement and attention, which the pupils repaid with lifted performances.

However, the Rosenthal experiment is *not* necessarily applicable to early selection, and more obviously relates to the advantages of *encouraging* children than it does to the consequences of *rejecting* those that seem to be of lower ability. What Rosenthal observed is a process that may go on *within* a school class, where the pupils constitute points of reference for each other. It may be that pupils in grammar and in modern schools respectively are *not* points of reference or comparison for each other, at least to the same extent as class mates. Whether the streams of a comprehensive school are more like class mates in this respect is, of course, a moot point. It is also worth noting that Rosenthal's observations are against the backcloth of a highly competitive culture, the American, rather than a setting more like Europe's, where 'success' is less widely and deeply sought and therefore 'failure' less poignant.

There is a study by Douglas which seems at first sight to confirm the application of Rosenthal's self-fulfilling prophecy to *streaming* (Douglas, 1964). It was conducted in primary schools upon a group of children born at the same time, that Douglas has traced from infancy to early adulthood. In this instance, the group was given IQ tests at seven and then again at eleven, Douglas felt his findings demonstrated that while individual children in the top streams of the primary schools improved on average (a little, but enough to be significant statistically), those in lower streams deteriorated. However, Horobin and others have shown him to be in error (Horobin *et al.*, 1967). The same result can be obtained by tracing the 'change' in individual scores in the reverse direction, that is from eleven to seven: high stream children 'improve' and low stream children 'deteriorate' as they grow *younger*! This makes a nonsense of Douglas' conclusions. They are an effect of his statistical techniques, not genuine. It is however, important to cite their unreliability since it is perhaps not as widely known as the study itself.

Another piece of evidence cited against early selection, especially in the early 1960s in England, is more impressive. It is the successes that secondary modern schools had with the introduction of O-level GCE (Pedley, 1963). This confirms that there are some pupils excluded by early selection who could have benefited from a more academic course. However, what O-level successes also show is that late developers are not completely suppressed by being sent to secondary modern school: the self-fulfilling prophecy may not operate.

This brings us to the second assumption implicit in Ford's conclusions from her comparison of comprehensive, modern and grammar schools: does early selection have flaws which even streamed comprehensive schools can lessen? If there is any educational merit in the recent moves towards multilateral schools in France and Belgium, and in experiments with the observation cycle in West Germany and the Netherlands, as well as in the great majority of interpretations of 'comprehensive schooling' in Britain, it must be at this point.

Early selection for different schools has been criticized for the margin of error that attends it, and the difficulty of putting things right later by transferring children from one school to another. It was the usual practice in England and Wales after the war to encourage the transfer of pupils between grammar school and secondary modern school if they later proved unsuitable for the course to which they were allocated at eleven. In some authorities there was a '13-plus' for late developers. If this arrangement had been used enough to remedy all the errors that selection at 11-plus entailed, at least 12 per cent of the joint grammar-modern intake would have exchanged courses (NFER, 1958). Nowhere near this number did so. In fact the introduction of O-level into secondary moderns is a sign of the failure of this transfer system. What militated against transfer between modern and grammar schools was the different content of the curricula in the parallel schools. There was also a social barrier, especially for those who faced the prospect of removal from the grammar school. Not least, there was an organizational barrier, between one school and another, between graduate staff and certificated staff.

Inside a comprehensive school that practises streaming, even from its first year, there is more flexibility for transfer than between parallel schools. It is the same body of teachers who determine where to place all the pupils, and control of transfer is likely to be in their hands to a greater degree, since the local authority is not involved and parents may well have less influence than over the transfer of pupils from one school to another. Whether the courses followed by different streams are as diverse as grammar and modern curricula depends very much on the individual school in England and Wales. In France and Belgium the nominal differences between 'sections' or 'sides' may be greater, but the actual courses have a common core for up to four years and this is predictable from school to school as it is not in England.

We can illustrate these propositions from two of the author's schools – Castle Town and Hinsley Mill (Bellaby, 1975). They started out as paired bilateral schools in the middle 1950s. Both had modern sides, but one had a grammar section, the other a technical section. The official intention was that pupils found to be in the wrong selective section a year or more after 11-plus, should be transferred to the other school. The provision of selective places in these two schools together was so generous in fact that they included most who would be in the top stream of a normal modern school along with the grammar school intake. Transfer took place very seldom, and then it was often to help each school's discipline problems. However, both schools, especially the technical/modern began to break down the distinction into sides and transfer pupils internally. This was helped by the fact that each had a relatively homogeneous staff. The grammar/modern had a high proportion of graduates, while the technical/modern staff was predominantly certificated. Of course the same fact may well have hindered transfers *between* schools.

By 1967 when the author observed them, each school was officially 'comprehensive'. As the head of the former technical/modern saw it, his school had grown into a comprehensive before it received the name. Not all would call it a full comprehensive, because it was streamed at entry into six ability streams taught by subject specialists, and two remedial classes. The other school had adopted a similar arrangement, indeed the top stream there was developed into an express stream (taking O-level in four rather than five years). Yet the rate of transfer between streams, especially in the former technical/modern school, was high, at least by the standards of the former practice of transfer between the two schools (or indeed between most grammar, technical and modern schools in the tripartite system). By the end of the third year, after which the original streams were modified to prepare for examination or terminal courses, 21·5 per cent of pupils in the former technical/modern and 16·5 per cent in the former grammar/modern had moved up at some point in their career; while 5·8 per cent and 5·1 per cent respectively had moved down. In the technical/modern a further 4·1 per cent had been moved both up and down and come to rest in their original stream, while 1·7 per cent of remedial children had been brought into the bottom ability stream. This means that about two thirds of pupils in the technical modern had stayed in the same stream and three quarters in the other school, far fewer than would have stayed put in grammar school or in secondary modern school.

A consequence of this flexibility should be that those who develop late, for example who fail 11-plus and afterwards improve, have a better chance of entering university from a comprehensive school than they have within a selective system. Neave's survey of students who went to university from comprehensive schools in 1968 shows this to be almost certainly the case (Neave, 1975a). No less than 15 per cent of the sample who went up from the longest-established comprehensives had failed 11-plus, rather more than the proportion who would have been misplaced aged 11-plus had they attended a modern rather than a comprehensive school, and surely far more than would have been transferred to grammar school at thirteen. Indeed, as Neave points out, three quarters of comprehensives allowed open access to their sixth forms, which enabled those who had failed crucial O-levels or had started in the wrong stream to remedy this and perhaps catch up with those whose career had proceeded at grammar school pace.

Another way of approaching the relative performance of comprehensive schools and the tripartite system is through results in external examinations and the rate of staying on beyond the statutory leaving age. Of these the second is by far the more reliable basis for comparison. Examination results reflect not only the performance of those pupils who take GCE but also the schools' policies towards entering children for examinations, which can be highly varied. Further, GCE results reflect the attainment of only a proportion of grammar school pupils, and a relatively low percentage of comprehensive pupils: they cannot measure a school's performance over the whole range of its courses.

The rate of staying on is not altogether independent of school policy. By the late 1950s grammar schools were viewing 'early leaving' (at fifteen) as incompatible with being a grammar school pupil. Since that time to stay beyond the leaving age has progressively become the norm in all types of school rather than the exception, though the raising of the leaving age to sixteen in 1973 (ROSLA) included within the compulsory ages the majority of those who would otherwise have stayed on voluntarily.

Table 5.1 takes the last official figures before ROSLA. It combines the remaining 'tripartite' schools, as if they constituted a system covering about 50 per cent of secondary pupils, and compares the rates of staying on to various ages within them with the corresponding rates for comprehensive schools. The rates are not actual but estimated. Actual rates for the age groups in question at each point of leaving are not available, and so we have computed each on the base of those pupils in comprehensive and tripartite schools respectively who were fourteen at the same time (January 1973).

Table 5.1 *Estimated rates of staying on beyond leaving age (before ROSLA) in the 'tripartite system' and in comprehensive schools, England and Wales*

	% leaving aged	January 1973		
	15 (over SLA)	16	17	18+
Tripartite schools	39·6	32·9	18·4	5·1
Comprehensive schools	37·0	31·3	15·6	4·6

At a straight reading the table shows remarkably little difference between the two systems, though it gives the edge to the tripartite system at every age of leaving. The main problem in reading the table straight is that the 'tripartite system' is not in fact sealed off from the comprehensive system. Grammar schools 'coexist' with comprehensives in many authorities, including schools supported by direct grants, which are in fact excluded from this table.

These grammar schools often, though not always 'cream off' children of the highest IQ within the catchment of the comprehensives. It is these children, of course, who are most likely to stay on, especially to seventeen or eighteen. It is impossible to state the amount of creaming off for the country as a whole, but we can estimate its order of magnitude. In 1973 30 per cent of pupils aged fourteen in the 'tripartite system' were attending selective schools (grammar or rarely technical). Standards for entry to grammar school varied from authority to authority. If we were to take it that anyone of 'above average ability' could go to grammar school, this would be conventionally regarded as 18 per cent of the age group (all above one standard deviation from the mean IQ). On that basis, in 1973 the tripartite system would have been receiving two thirds more pupils of above average ability than it was 'entitled to', while, presuming that its gain was a direct loss to comprehensive schools, the comprehensive system would have been receiving about a third of its 'entitlement'. This would be an exaggeration, since the average admission rate to selective schools was nearer to 25 per cent of the age group before comprehensive reorganization was seriously underway. By such a standard each of the percentages in the table should be adjusted as follows: for the tripartite system *reduce* by one fifth, for the comprehensive system *increase* by one third. If such a speculation is valid, the comprehensive system would have a decisively higher rate of staying on at every age than the tripartite system: at age 15, but over school leaving age (SLA) 49 per cent as opposed to 32 per cent, at age 16 42 per cent as opposed to 26 per cent, at age 17 21 per cent as opposed to 16 per cent, and at age 18+ 6 per cent as opposed to 4 per cent. Perhaps it would be better to leave the impression that, given that *some* creaming off does occur, the rates of staying on in comprehensive schools are far from discreditable.

Since most of these practised streaming in some form, internal streaming must be less rigid than separating pupils into different schools by their ability. Even so streaming in a comprehensive can have varied effects on pupils' aspirations, depending on how flexible it is.

Of the three highly comparable schools studied by this author, one kept a relatively high proportion of its pupils in the same stream from entry (Castle Town), while the others promoted and demoted in quite large numbers and regularly. A greater emphasis in lessons on 'getting on with work', and more criticism of standards of achievement went along with the more flexible streaming. This greater flexibility had two measurable effects on pupils' aspirations: first, it meant that a somewhat higher percentage of pupils in the bottom two of six streams in the two schools that were flexible, wished to stay after fifteen and also aspired to take external exams (GCE or CSE) than their counterparts in the relatively inflexible school; secondly, it entailed a higher proportion in the two flexible schools who looked to some way out of taking employment offered in or near the town where they lived, in other words to marriage, the army or (occasionally) football or pop music. This is consistent with the theory that if you hold out hopes longer for pupils and encourage (or push) them to achieve more forcibly, you create higher aspirations, but also a tendency to opt out, perhaps in order to neutralize the sense of failure felt by some in any competition.

Whether the *abolition* of streaming inside comprehensive schools will allow talent to develop further is debateable. There has been much research on the relative educational merits of mixed ability and streamed classes, especially in the United States and Sweden. A fairly up to date review of American research by one of its main practitioners, Passow, reveals disappointingly inconclusive results (Yates, 1968). Swedish research is a little more positive. For example, Carlsson found that, while by the end of the seventh grade (age fourteen) pupils following academic courses did better in streams than in mixed ability classes, by the end of the eighth grade there was little to choose between them, and throughout children in practical courses did better in mixed ability classes (cited in Yates, 1968).

However, another Swedish study (by Rudberg) showed that the attitudes of children towards each other in mixed ability classes were more unfavourable than in ability streams (cited in Yates, 1968). As will be seen later, a study by Lacey in a grammar school that was not streamed in the first year suggests how unfavourable stereotypes might have emerged of some pupils among their peers and teachers (Lacey, 1970). This appears to have been an informal process of 'academic differentiation', not dissimilar to that observed by Rosenthal. Thus the *mix* of abilities in one class does *not* necesarily prevent selection of a kind.

Further, selection for different kinds of schools or courses is aimed at identifying 'talent' in strictly academic terms. If an *informal* process of differentiation takes its place – like an open contest – children may be able to trade on a variety of advantages, including the favour of teachers and fellow pupils. Academic talent may thus become *less* decisive for success at school if the 'mixed ability' approach takes over. A long term trend of this kind attracted much criticism in American comment on the high school in the 1950s and '60s. For example, Coleman believed that the high school had become the focus of 'adolescent society', with an emphasis on athletic prowess, good looks and charm and getting into the right circles, rather than academic success (Coleman, 1961). His research (in ten schools) concentrated on students' perceptions of school, and, since a discrepancy between the official (academic) culture of the school and its pupils' informal culture is a common finding, he may have overstated the significance of the trend he found. But the fact remains that reforms originally aimed at altering the means by which academic goals are reached can have the effect of redefining the educational enterprise.

(ii) *Can academic differentiation be abolished?*

The move away from selective schools and ability grouping in Europe *is* significant; it is not a change in form that leaves the content untouched, a mere decanting of *old* wine into *new* bottles. At the same time, it would be mistaken to suppose that the present trend against academic differentiation will *abolish* this practice. Comprehensive schools and mixed ability groups at best put off the separation of pupils into different courses. Throughout most of Europe and in the USSR, entry to higher education is by selection or qualifications not the student's free choice. Minimum qualifications are required, and even these may not guarantee a place. Other institutions of further education require qualifications and favourable references from school, and so do employers. Confronted with the need to gain employment and knowing that the kind of further education or job they want requires qualification in certain subjects, *pupils* will differentiate themselves, even if teachers do not select or guide them.

In the United States access to higher education is far more open than in Europe, and yet, as is well-documented by sociologists, schools 'cool-out' the ambitions to go to college of those who might be academically unsuitable. 'Cooling out' happens at two levels. First many schools have a counselling service which periodically tests pupils' vocational aptitudes and offers advice on the election of courses. Secondly, as their expectations start to form, pupils group themselves into college-goers and non-college-goers and their friendships help reinforce their expectations. Needless to say, we ought to add a third level, since what the counselling service and the pupils themselves know of their aptitudes is largely a reflection of the way teachers have judged their performances in class and in written work, and the grades that have been awarded.

Cooling out is an *unintended* consequence of the arrangement of American high schools. Many counsellors would disagree that they offer *advice*, let alone shape pupils' choices for them. In California, Clark studied a school which epitomizes this approach (Clark, 1961). It was an 'open-door' to all who wished to gain access to university or liberal arts college, but had failed to do so after senior high school. After two years of study there, students could pass on to higher education proper. However, during those two years the school deterred a large proportion of hitherto ambitious students from pursuing their original intentions. Counselling – 'non-directive' of course – was the principal instrument (see also Cicourel and Kitsuse, 1963).

In England there is detailed documentation of how, in spite of mixed ability grouping in the first year of a grammar school, teachers and boys in interplay sorted pupils out into the able and the less able. Lacey's study was conducted in a school which began streaming in the second year with a view eventually to putting some boys in for O-level GCE at fifteen, some at sixteen, and leaving the rest to gain lesser qualifications or quit school with none at all. Clearly the *informal* academic differentiation of pupils in the first year anticipates streaming in the second. Nevertheless, it is a consequence of mixed ability grouping that teachers did not intend, and so it bears comparison with the findings from

102

American comprehensive schools and the 'open-door' college (Lacey, 1970).

It should not be supposed that counsellors and teachers set out to separate the sheep from the goats or even that they are hypocrites. Another English study, this time in a comprehensive school, shows that a 'progressive' humanities department, teaching the sociology of the family to fourth year classes, felt that it should disregard the school's streaming and teach the same material in the same way to all classes (Keddie, 1971). They gave all pupils cards with definitions of terms and facts on them, and conducted similar question and answer discussions in class. But an upper stream observed by Keddie played the game the teacher's way by learning the cards and answering questions within the framework they provided. The lower stream she observed posed questions from their own experience of family life and arrangements, and the teacher responded by asserting the definitions and facts on the cards and suppressing the 'noise' that pupils caused. In short, the teacher did not treat the upper and lower streams on equal terms. And the example contains a clue as to why he did not. He worked within a concept, rather a narrow one, of what was proper knowledge about his subject, the family.

We can say that Keddie's teacher ought to have listened to the lower stream's questions, to have allowed them to talk about their own experiences and to have built his lesson around them. Ultimately, however, teaching and also research depend upon a concept of what is 'proper knowledge'. That concept may be arbitrary. But perpetual open-mindedness unfortunately amounts to empty-mindedness: there can be no enquiry without questions framed by a theory, and teachers deceive themselves if they think that they are not attempting to shape pupils' minds, however gently. Those pupils who for any reason at all, whether native ability, the way they were brought up, or sheer cunning, learn to play the teacher's game, are likely to get better grades or be advised to follow academic courses. Others will be judged less able and diverted to non-academic courses when the opportunity arises.

This educational basis for academic differentiation is reinforced by the links that pupils and their parents will forge between job-opportunities and their current school performance.

Thus it is common to find as did this writer, that by early adolescence boys and girls have formed quite 'realistic' concepts of their future occupations. As Ford points out, much research into choice of occupation by young adolescents has equated the low ambition of the less academically successful with their having failed 11-plus (Ford, 1969). However, in the three comprehensive schools I studied, much as in Ford's one comprehensive school, pupils in the third year were likely to think they might get a job in management or become a professional by twenty-five if they were in the top streams, but the nearer they were to the bottom stream, the more likely they were to say that manual work (for boys) or a clerical job or just 'housewife' (for girls) was how they saw themselves. Since there was a close correspondence between these expectations and whether or not they felt they would be taking O-level or CSE examinations and staying at school beyond fifteen, the then legal leaving age, it is clear that school performance plays a prominent part in the concept that children have in secondary school of their future careers. Contrary to popular imagination, young teenagers seldom think they will become footballers, singers or models. Their more mundane ambitions arise from academic differentiation (whether formal or informal) and reinforce that process.

The egalitarian argument

We have spoken of 'wastage of talent' in educational terms. This waste is often represented as *social* in origin. It was well established by research in the period between the wars as well as after, that middle class children had more chance of getting into grammar school, of staying on at the legal leaving age and of going to university than working class children. The more prestigious the fathers' occupation, and the higher his and/or his wife's educational level, the greater the likelihood that the child would succeed in climbing the educational ladder. Being a girl, especially a working class girl made things more difficult still. After the war places in grammar school and in university were increased, but class differentials within the institutions persisted. Working class children, especially boys, had improved their grasp on grammar school places between the wars. After the war middle class children took a more than proportionate share of the increase in grammar school places. Until the expansion of higher education in the 1960s, the ratio of workers' children there to the children of middle class parents remained virtually unchanged over fifty years (Little and Westergaard, 1964).

Of course what these observations conceal is the *expansion* of the middle classes and their changing complexion. The old middle class of small businessmen gave way to a bigger, mixed bag of professionals employed by the state or in industry, of administrators, managers and clerical workers. The tendency for this group once established to take more than their share of places in schools and universities has been observed in USSR, in spite of a self-conscious attempt there to favour the children of workers and peasants. It is also characteristic of the United States. Thus two countries with comprehensive secondary schools, one with a socialist ideology, reveal the same pattern of class differentials in access to education as England, with its selective system.

It would be surprising if the comprehensive reform in England had made it as likely that a labourer's child would go to university as a doctor's child. However, much of the literature gives the impression that it is *selection per se* that puts the working class children at a disadvantage. Thus it is common to find that when comprehensive schools stream their intake they inadvertently fill the top streams with middle class children and the bottom with sons and daughters of unskilled and semi-skilled workers (see Bellaby, 1975; Ford, 1969; Holly, 1965). Ford and Holly point out that this practice is not radically different from the old 11-plus (though as we have seen streaming usually allows movement from course to course more readily than does segregation into separate schools). But it does not follow that streaming (or 11-plus) puts working class boys and girls at *more* of a disadvantage than open competition among children of all abilities. In short selection may not be the culprit at all.

As we saw, selection at 11-plus was criticized by psychologists for the margin of error it entailed and the fact that institutional barriers between schools made many errors irreversible. 11-plus was open to criticism from a more overtly 'social' stance by sociologists and some government reports. The theme was the uneven distribution of opportunities for higher level education among the social classes. There were two sets of findings. The first concerned the relatively low probability that an unskilled worker's child would gain a place at grammar school. The second was the wastage of ability because of 'early leaving' from grammar schools, mainly workers' children. The second finding has a different implication from the first. In the government report on Early Leaving measured ability is taken as given, and working class boys of ability are shown to leave earlier than their middle class counterparts (CACE, 1954). On the other hand, a careful comparative study of 11-plus selection in Middlesbrough and S.W. Hertfordshire by Floud, Halsey and Martin shows that able workers' boys are as likely to get into grammar schools as able middle class boys (Floud *et al.*, 1957). The authors showed that 'ability' is unevenly distributed among social classes – a familiar finding, but suggest that ability depends upon the home background of the child and the way this background interacts with the school, not entirely upon inheritance.

Before the war it was commonly supposed that poor families were at a disadvantage for education because their home conditions were unhealthy and the income of their parents could not readily support the longer education at the grammar school. Much emphasis was placed on free or subsidized school meals, on free milk, on school health services – anything that could compensate for material deprivations at home. Floud found scope for further improvement here in Middlesbrough, but Hertfordshire suggested that the trend was towards higher incomes and better housing and standards of home hygiene and nutrition. What would now separate workers' families from those of the middle classes was values, beliefs, rules of conduct, which would provide children with the base from which they might succeed at school. Floud also suggested that grammar schools had a middle class aura, which militated against working class boys. From all this it follows that inequalities of opportunity are not to be removed by the selection of children on ability at 11-plus.

To some environmental theorists schooling seems inherently discriminatory: it always favours the child from a more favourable environment, so that to extend schooling is to pour good money after bad. Others pin their faith on 'compensatory' education, for example nursery schools in deprived urban areas, since they believe that equality of opportunity depends on large scale social engineering through the school. From this position comprehensive schooling is a form of compensatory education.

Neave has attempted to show that comprehensive schools in England and Wales may have already improved the chances of working class children to enter university (Neave, 1975). In his sample of undergraduates from comprehensive schools who entered university in 1968, he found that there was a higher percentage (38 per cent) from working class backgrounds than in the student body as a whole (28 per cent). Unfortunately, perhaps because of the small budget on which so much research on English comprehensives has been conducted, Neave lacked adequate control groups. In particular, he did not know the class composition by 11-plus results of the total intake of the comprehensive schools from which his university sample had sprung. As a result it is impossible to be certain whether the relatively large proportion of working class students among the sample reflects a particularly *small* percentage of 11-plus successes of middle class origin entering comprehensive schools, or instead the special opportunities and encouragement that the schools might give to working class pupils. Neave notes that a particularly high proportion of 11-plus *failures* who went on to university were working class (44 per cent). It is very probable that they would not have had this chance had they gone to a modern school; on the other hand, nor would the middle class 11-plus failures. In spite of Neave's argument that being middle class does *not* favour the progress of a child within a comprehensive school, it is clear that more of the middle class children who failed 11-plus fought their way through to university than of their counterparts who were working class. For what it is worth, there is even evidence in his tables that allows a contrary interpretation, for many of the ex-comprehensive school undergraduates came from LEAs that had abolished 11-plus, and yet the class-composition of this group was precisely similar to that of the 11-plus successes. Thus Neave's findings on the class background of his sample are inconclusive.

If we are to go beyond this impasse, more than a generous research budget is needed. We have to theorize the conditions in which comprehensive schools might improve the chances of working class children entering university, and be prepared to test our theory at its critical points.

The least plausible beginning is to assume that 'comprehensive schools' form a homogeneous class distinct from grammar and modern schools; that they have 'goals' all their own, which are followed by all their members. Yet several commentators, including Neave, come perilously close to this position. Thus Neave sees length of establishment as a more or less adequate criterion of comprehensiveness. He calls recently reorganized schools 'crypto-grammar', but it is not unlikely that earlier schools might be characterized as 'crypto-secondary-modern', operating within an environment still dominated by academic achievements. Clearly how schools operate depends in a complex way upon the definitions (often competing) of staff with varied training and experience, the strategy of the head, and the expectations of the 'public' and education authorities. Even if these concur, there is yet scope for pupils to define the school in different ways depending on their concept of their future in the labour market.

The absence of a clearly defined entity 'comprehensive schooling' is one problem, another is that no school can be completely independent of the wider society, far less shape society as it wills. The inequalities that lead middle class children to do better at school than working class children are not produced by the school alone; they are embedded in capitalist relations of production. If the prime function of schooling in capitalism is to sort out children by their personal characteristics and to inculcate attitudes and behaviour that will ensure that they accept their roles in the production system, we must expect middle class children, already prepared by their parents, to receive preference for positions requiring 'leadership' and 'dependability', and we should not be surprised to find different treatment meted out to those chosen than to those who are rejected for these roles. Even if there is a measure of social mobility, that is even if a proportion of working class children enter white collar and professional tracks in school, the basic relation of education to capitalism is unaltered, since these children will be socialized out of their class background and into their future status. Of far more significance would be a school regime that worked counter to both middle class and working class background, for this could drive a progressive wedge between schooling and capitalism. Needless to say the impact of a school like this on university entrance would depend on there being a similar contradiction between higher education and capitalism; otherwise the outflow from the school to university might be reduced to zero!

It is not impossible for a school to develop in the way we have indicated, and the scope for a comprehensive school of mixed class composition to do so is plainly greater than for a more middle class grammar school or more working class secondary modern. It is difficult: the author's three schools adopted regimes in class that differentiated between the top stream of potential sixth formers and university entrants, and the lower streams, many of whom were destined to leave early and go into factory or routine office work. I observed the top and the fifth of six streams in the third year in each of the schools for a week's lessons apiece. The upper stream was more likely to be involved in discussion by the teacher, was given more homework and classwork that demanded self-direction, and was also censured when it failed to behave or complete work 'responsibly'. The lower stream was the target of efforts, not always successful, to prevent movement about the room, to suppress noise and to keep up application to routine tasks, such as copying maps. There was a more than accidental resemblance between the classroom setting and the large factory or open plan office. Ironically, it was the ex-grammar school (Castle Town) that differentiated least between the two streams, by being relatively permissive to both. The school which tried hardest to be progressive (Cross Street), had a regime, especially with the lower stream, which was widely at variance with that advocated by the head and the staff committee on rewards and punishments, and was most punitive of all. If such practices are widespread, it is hard to see in what important sense comprehensive schools do anything but reinforce the inequalities that exist in capitalist society. The same conclusion must apply even if, as is by no means established, a slightly higher proportion of working class children are in higher streams and pass through the sixth form and into university from comprehensives than do so from selective schools.

The communitarian argument

(i) *The mixture of social differences*

'Social integration' was a self-conscious purpose of most of the early comprehensive schools in England and remains a goal within the reorganized comprehensive system today. However, in the earlier schools, at least up to the middle to late 1960s, the instrument that was expected to further social integration was the house or house group. This was a vertical division within the school which co-existed with the normal horizontal divisions between age groups and between streams or bands of ability within age groups.

Ford's comprehensive school had a house system which incorporated each child into a registration group of about thirty pupils of the same age but differing ability (Ford, 1969). As we have seen the same children were streamed for lessons. In response to Ford's questions about their best friends, the vast majority named class mates not members of the same house registration group, and few could recall their friends' houses. From this it would appear that house groups set, as it were, at 90 degrees to the principal basis of differentiation by age and ability in the school, had little social significance for pupils.

Ford also points out that children might form friendships on two *social* bases, one their class of origin, the other aspirations (to stay at school or leave, for future status) that they shared. In the comprehensive school, in contrast to the grammar school, friendships tended to form by class background rather than common aspirations. Ironically the grammar school did a better job of mixing the social classes than did the comprehensive school, though of course friendships *were* differentiated on a social basis, what we might call *future* social class. It may be added that in spite of each school's co-educational teaching, friendships, like aspirations, were sharply separated between girls and boys.

It must be said that Ford's findings may not be typical of comprehensive schools. The three that this author studied in detail were all slightly more 'modern' in that they did not have or had abandoned experiments with a house system. The taught form and the registration group were identical. However, all three schools were streamed and friendships were closely allied to both stream and sex, as in Ford's school. The principal difference is that in all three aspiration for the future was a far more significant factor in friendship than class of origin. Indeed in one school, social class had no overall impact on choice of friends, perhaps because this school was predominantly working class in composition, and there was no marked tendency for the middle class pupils to monopolize the top streams as at the other schools. In all three schools boys and girls who wanted to stay on and who aspired to professional or managerial careers tended to choose each other, even if they were in different forms. It was only in the most working class school that children in the same stream mixed indifferently with others of the same and different social aspirations. This may possibly have been due to treating each form as a 'tutor group' welded together by the same teacher over its period in the school and sharing a number of extra-curricular activities in common as well as lessons. Whether Ford's finding or this writer's is the more typical does not alter the generalization that friendships in comprehensives do tend to form around class, whether class of origin or anticipated future class (see also Eggleston, 1974).

Social forces, such as class and aspirations and sex, seem too powerful to be offset by such devices as house groups or co-education so far as choice of best friends is concerned. However, it has been argued, with some justification, that teaching *boys and girls* together helps to make them more comprehensible to each other and less ill at ease in each other's presence. If comprehensive schools revert to mixed ability grouping on a large scale, classes, both of origin and aspiration, may be mixed together to a greater extent than was the case in the schools studied by Ford and this writer. This may not promote 'mixed' friendships any more than coeducation induces boys and girls of the same age to choose each other as 'best friends' rather than pick others of the opposite sex a little younger or older as 'girlfriends' or 'boyfriends'. But that is arguably different from creating some sense of community among people with social differences.

(ii) *Stereotypes as barriers to communication*

One indicator of the creation of such 'community' would be the reduction of such hostile stereotypes as social classes (or racial groups) might have of each other.

A study by Himmelweit and others suggested in the early 1950s that while grammar school pupils viewed society as a ladder up which anyone could climb, modern school pupils saw it as two classes polarized against each other (Himmelweit *et al.*, 1952). An early study of a comprehensive school by Miller indicated that such characteristic differences in the outlook of middle and working class people might be narrowed by their being taught in a common school. Miller clearly envisaged the reduction of class conflict (Miller, 1961). Comprehensive schools are thus expected to inculcate the grammar school and middle class view of society as a ladder rather than two camps opposed to each other. Ford took up this idea and gathered from pupils in her different schools the various images of society that they entertained (Ford, 1969). Her model of different images was fourfold. She distinguished on the one hand dichotomous (or two class) images from hierarchical (or ladder) images, and on the other hand, those images which legitimated the perceived state of affairs from those which attacked it as illegitimate.

Whatever the school, middle class pupils are more likely to choose the hierarchy image and working class pupils the dichotomy image; further, girls favour the ladder model more than do boys. If we confine attention to boys in comparing the schools, it appears that grammar school boys are more likely to accept or legitimate the class structure as they see it than are boys in the secondary modern, and that while boys in the B to D streams of the comprehensive resemble the modern school boys in this respect, those in the A stream are only a little more like the grammar school boys. The ladder image is preferred to the two-class mode by grammar school boys and A stream comprehensive boys in about equal proportions (two thirds to one third), while the boys in the secondary modern and in the B to D streams of the comprehensive closely resemble each other in being divided 50/50 between the two images.

Thus, once again Ford's comprehensive school shatters an

expectation formed by the advocates of comprehensive schooling. Her suggestion that streaming in the comprehensive operates in this respect much like the division between the grammar and the modern school seems inescapable. However, it does not follow from this that the abolition of streaming will necessarily make everyone adopt a 'ladder' view of the class structure. This would demand a radical change in the English cultural tradition, which the politics of the 1970s suggest is unrealistic. Since the 1950s and early 1960s era of centre politics in which the function of comprehensive schooling as a mixer of classes and healer of social divisions was conceived, class divisions in industry and between political parties have sharpened. Indeed dichotomy models seem to have been espoused on both sides. Since these more or less correspond to reality as we have depicted it, it would be strange indeed to conclude this section by agreeing with the comprehensive reformers who wish to see children adopting ladder (or American style 'contest') imagery of the social structure.

6

Conclusion

'Comprehensive schooling' has proved difficult to define. In England it is usually taken to mean educating all children of secondary school age in an area in one school. This may involve exposing pupils of different backgrounds and abilities to each other (as in thinly populated areas), or it may lead to a 'one-class' school that reflects the predominantly middle class or working class composition of its catchment.

Another feature of 'comprehensive schooling' is that it delays the separation of pupils into different courses. Some Western European countries have, at some stage in their reform of selective schools, introduced a common core of studies in the first few years of the selective schools, in order that pupils might be reassessed and transferred late to the school that fits their abilities. If we hesitate to call this reform 'comprehensive', we might pause about a common school that is divided into sections (a 'multilateral' like the French CES), and even more so about an English comprehensive that is so streamed, banded or setted in the early years that pupils may be taking quite dissimilar courses.

However, the organizational form of a school does not guarantee the content of the education it offers. This depends upon how teachers – and also parents and pupils – define the educational process, and which definition (if any) prevails. Because reorganization has meant the enforced co-operation of teachers with different training and experience, and because influential parents have often demanded 'academic' schooling for their children, the comprehensive school has sometimes become a battleground of competing interests. Even if the parties agree, they are under constraint to introduce 'academic differentiation' within the comprehensive school. When it is in equilibrium with capitalist relations of production, the school helps reproduce the social conditions for continued economic activity – that is, it sorts pupils and prepares them to accept their future work roles. Even in mixed ability classes, individuals are likely to be treated differently: to have much or little expected of them, to be encouraged or repressed.

Does this make the educational, egalitarian and communitarian aims of the advocates of comprehensive schooling into empty dreams? The answer to this question must be complex. There seems sound evidence that comprehensive schools permit the identification of 'late developers' and their allocation, however late, to courses that fit their abilities. This is true even of streamed comprehensives. On the other hand, it is a mistake to suppose that schooling alone can repair the inequalities, the repression and the alienation which are inherent in capitalist relations of production.

Schooling has *relative autonomy* within capitalism. It *may* contradict the logic of capital accumulation. Usually this is because schooling is slow to adjust, as indeed are all institutions. In education, this lag is most obvious in the supply of technical skills to the labour market. Again and again, schooling either under or over produces, or fails to give relevant training. In principle, schooling can advance *ahead* of capital accumulation. Should it do so, the contradiction is heightened. If schooling promises equality that is manifestly withheld by relations of production, it can promote political action by those who are disadvantaged. An example may be that liberal education and steps towards the desegregation of high schools in the United States, helped feed the Black Civil Rights Movement. However, the threads linking

115

educational change and social revolution are easily broken. This is clear from the backlash that followed, in which educationists justified racial inequality by claiming that it was founded on differences in IQ which were genetic. So is the class struggle fought within education, as it is in production and in politics.

In England, comprehensivization has become an important political issue, at all levels, from Parliament to the grass roots. Many educationists see politics as an intrusion – at best a necessary evil to provide the will and resources to modify existing institutions. However, whether or not educational reform enters the legitimate political arena, it is likely to precipitate conflicts of interest and value among teachers and others directly involved. We have argued that not only the legitimate politics of the comprehensive reform, but also the debates in educational circles are rooted in changing class relations. The first pressure for reform (in the late 1950s and early 1960s) expressed the dilemma posed for the ever-expanding lower and middle echelons of the 'new middle classes', by narrow access to educational qualifications in the selective school system. The hardening of party political positions in the middle 1960s and especially at local government level, may have reflected a new alignment in the debate – this time between the working class and the middle class. The intensity of the struggle was reflected not so much in national as in local politics. The national leadership of the Conservative Party resisted constant pressure from its rank and file to take issue with the abolition of 11-plus and the erosion of the grammar schools because opinion polls and party intelligence indicated wide popular support for Labour's policy on secondary education. The main battles were fought locally between party groups on the Councils, between pressure groups of teachers and of parents. Which party controlled a particular local education authority was crucial to the progress it made with preparing and implementing plans for comprehensive schooling. During the 1960s the fortunes of the parties in local government fluctuated, so much so that few remained in the hands of the same party throughout the decade. In the crucial period of a year or two after the issue of the Ministerial Circular 10/65, Labour control made a rapid start with comprehensivization probable, while Conservative control made delay, over a prolonged period, equally probable. Party control at

116

this time strongly reflected the class composition of the local electorate. While class composition did not prevent many authorities from reverting to the other party at subsequent elections, it did seem to impede a complete reversal of educational policy.

However, the relationship between the strength in numbers of the local working class and the local education authority's progress with reform may not be so simple as this implies. A dozen solidly Labour and strongly working class authorities were slow to comprehensivize. We have proposed the tentative hypothesis that they represent the lack of education-consciousness characteristic of much of the so-called 'traditional' working class: it is not accidental that all but two are Northern industrial towns, and that one of the others is the most working class of all London boroughs (Newham). Conversely, pressure for comprehensive reform may have come from the more consumption-conscious 'affluent' workers, who, we suggest might see in education not an opportunity for individual advancement, but rather a service (or commodity) that all have the right to enjoy without status distinction.

In the 1970s reorganization has continued, and even now it is incomplete. From the Ford strike of 1969 to the miners' strike that brought down the Conservative government in 1974, conflict in industry was at the centre of the political arena, with the government increasingly implicated. It is only the mutual involvement of unions and government in the politics of the social contract that holds at bay a repetition of this situation. Comprehensive reform has slipped out of the public eye. For the most part, the Conservative Party has capitulated. The struggle has moved within the schools, and concerns their internal organization, the curriculum and methods of teaching and of social control. However progressive values like the playing down of assessment and selection and the celebration of choice and variety, the deprecation of streaming and the advocacy of mixed ability grouping can be a mask for practices of a quite contrary nature. It is possible that England is drifting towards a redefinition of the educational enterprise in terms of 'contest mobility'; if so this will move English education nearer to the American model without altering the fundamental relationship between schooling and society, or the inequalities on which that relationship hinges.

At the time of writing, the Labour Government is preoccupied with persuading and, if necessary, forcing recalcitrant LEAs to adopt comprehensive schools. Their efforts may increase permanently the control that central government has over local education. There is wide diversity in LEA schemes for reorganization and among individual comprehensive schools. Central control alone can reduce this and lead to the uniformity which characterizes Sweden and France.

However, it is arguable that only people who confine the term 'comprehensive schooling' to the common school, can welcome the imposition of uniformity from the centre. Many who believe that the comprehensive school should be the focus of the particular aspirations of the local community it serves, claim that control must be devolved to its teachers, pupils and parents. Whether local or central control could advance *equality* further is less easy to determine. We have suggested that schooling will have an impact on inequality only by divorcing itself from the demands of capitalism: its content must not be Utopian, however, and neither 'middle class' nor 'working class', but instead develop all talents to the highest degree, and provide its pupils with the means to analyse capitalist society and their situation within it. Since the state ultimately serves the interests of capital, centralization should be resisted. On the other hand, the involvement of parents, pupils and teachers in defining the aims and content of education does not guarantee radical schooling. The development of comprehensive schooling must be guided by a theory of educational change, which people involved in the struggle to overcome inequality and divisiveness within society must modify as experience demands. From an academic point of view, *research* is sadly lacking in English comprehensive schooling. Its absence is important, but less so than that of a theory of how the comprehensive reform has emerged and where it might evolve.

References and
name index

The numbers in italics following each entry refer to page numbers within this book.

Althusser, L. (1972) Ideology and ideological state apparatuses. In B. Cosin (ed.) *Education: Structure and Society*. Harmondsworth: Penguin. *34*

Anderson, E. (1973) *The Disabled Schoolchild: A Study of Integration in Primary Schools*. London: Methuen. *18*

Aries, P. (1973) *Centuries of Childhood*. Harmondsworth: Penguin. *35*

Banks, O. (1955) *Parity and Prestige in English Secondary Education*. London: Routledge and Kegan Paul. *40*

Barker, R. and Gump, P. (1964) *Big School, Small School*. Stanford: California University Press. *75*

Batley, R., O'Brien, O. and Parris, H. (1970) *Going Comprehensive*. London: Routledge and Kegan Paul. *60, 68*

Bellaby, P. (1974) The distribution of deviance among 13/14 year old students. In J. Eggleston (ed.) *Contemporary Research in the Sociology of Educaton*. London: Methuen. *88*

Bellaby, P. (1975) *Attitudinal Measurements of the Effect of Systems*

of Social Control in Different Secondary Schools. Unpublished
Ph.D. thesis: University of Cambridge. *78, 80, 105ff, 80–89,
96–97, 104, 109–111*

Benn, C. and Simon, B. (1972) *Halfway There.* 2nd edition.
Harmondsworth: Penguin. *12, 33, 92*

Berg, L. (1968) *Risinghill: the Death of a Comprehensive School.*
Harmondsworth: Penguin. *80*

Bowles, S. and Gintis, H. (1976) *Schooling in Capitalist America.*
London: Routledge and Kegan Paul. *34*

Boyson, R. (1975) *Parental Choice: Participation and Freedom in
Education.* London: Conservative Political Centre. *17ff, 24*

Braverman, H. (1974) *Labor and Monopoly Capital.* New York:
Monthly Review Press. *41*

Bronfenbrenner, U. (1974) *Two Worlds of Childhood: US and USSR.*
Harmondsworth: Penguin. *36*

Campaign for Comprehensive Education (1971, 1972) *Comprehensive
Reorganization Surveys* (edited by C. Benn) London. *12, 65*

Central Advisory Council for Education (1954) *Early Leaving.*
London. *106*

Cicourel, A. and Kitsuse, J. (1963) *The Educational Decision-
Makers.* New York: Bobbs-Merrill. *102*

Clark, B. (1961) The 'cooling out' function in higher education.
In A. Halsey *et al.* (ed.) *Education Economy and Society.* Glencoe,
Illinois: Free Press. *102*

Coleman, J. (1961) *Adolescent Society.* Glencoe, Illinois: Free Press.
101

Collins, R. (1972) Functional and conflict theories of educational
stratification. In B. Cosin (ed.) *Education: Structure and Society.*
Harmondsworth: Penguin. *34*

Council of Europe (1970) Council for Cultural Cooperation.
School Systems: A Guide. 2nd edition. Strasbourg. *28*

Cox, C. and Dyson, A. (ed.) (1971) *The Black Papers on Education.*
London: Davis Poynter. *17*

Cox, C. and Boyson R. (ed.) (1975) *Black Paper 1975.* London:
Dent. *17*

Crozier, M. (1966) France. In Sturmthal, A. (ed.) *White Collar
Trade Unionism.* University of Illinois Press. *52*

Donnison, D. *et al.* (1965) *Social Policy and Administration.*
London: George, Allen and Unwin. *59*

Douglas, J. (1964) *The Home and the School.* London: MacGibbon
and Kee. *94*

Eggleston, J. (1974) Some environmental correlates of extended secondary education in England. In J. Eggleston (ed.) *Contemporary Research in the Sociology of Education*. London: Methuen. *111*

Fenwick, I. (1976) *The Comprehensive School 1944-1970: The Politics of Secondary School Reorganization*. London: Methuen. *54*

Floud, J., Halsey A. and Martin J. (1957) *Social Class and Educational Opportunity*. London: Heinemann. *106*

Ford, J. (1969) *Social Class and the Comprehensive School*. London: Routledge and Kegan Paul. *92, 104, 105, 110, 111, 112ff, 113*

Fraser, W. (1971) *Reforms and Restraints in Modern French Education*. London: Routledge and Kegan Paul. *49*

Goldthorpe, J. *et al.* (1969) *The Affluent Worker in the Class Structure*. Cambridge University Press. *72-3*

Hargreaves, D. (1967) *Social Relations in a Secondary School*. London: Routledge and Kegan Paul. *83*

Heidenheimer, A. (1974) The politics of educational reform: explaining the different outcomes of school comprehensivization attempts in Sweden and West Germany. *Comparative Education Reivew* 18: 148. *50*

Himmelweit, H. *et al.* (1952) The views of adolescents on some aspects of class structure. *British Journal of Sociology* 3: 148. *112*

Holly, D. (1965) Profiting from a comprehensive school: class, sex and ability. *British Journal of Sociology* 16: 150. *92, 105*

Horobin, G. *et al.* (1967) The social differentiation of ability. *Sociology* 1: 113. *94*

Illich, I. (1973) *Deschooling Society*. Harmondsworth: Penguin. *17*

Jencks, C. *et al.* (1972) *Inequality: A Reassessment of the Effect of Family and Schooling in America*. New York: Basic Books. *34*

Katz, M. (1971) *Class, Bureaucracy and the Schools*. New York: Praeger. *38*

Keddie, N. (1971) Classroom knowledge. In M. F. D. Young (ed.) *Knowledge and Control*. London: Collier Macmillan. *87, 103*

Keddie, N. (1973) *Tinker, Tailor: the Myth of Cultural Deprivation*. Harmondsworth: Penguin. *22*

Lacey, C. (1970) *Hightown Grammar*. Manchester University Press. *42, 83, 100, 103*

Lawson, J. and Silver, H. (1973) *A Social History of Education in England*. London: Methuen. *38*

Little, A. and Westergaard, J. (1964) The trend of class differentials in educational opportunity in England and Wales. *British Journal of Sociology* 15: 301. *21, 105*

Marsden, D. (1971) *Politicians, Equality and Comprehensives*. Fabian Tract 411. London: Fabian Society. *19*

Miller, T. (1961) *Values in the Comprehensive School*. University of Birmingham: Institute of Education. Educational Monographs No. 5. *112*

Neave, G. (1975a) *How They Fared*. London: Routledge and Kegan Paul. *17, 97, 107*

Neave, G. (1975b) The reform of secondary education in France. *Forum* 17: 58. *31*

National Foundation for Educational Research (1958) *Allocation to Secondary Education*. Slough: NFER. *95*

Parkinson, M. (1970) *The Labour Party and the Organisation of Secondary Education 1918–1965*. London: Routledge and Kegan Paul. *60*

Paulston, R. (1968) *Educational Change in Sweden*. New York: Teachers College Press. *49*

Pedley, R. (1963) *The Comprehensive School*. Harmondsworth: Penguin. *59, 95*

Peschek, D. and Brand, J. (1966) *Policies and Politics in Secondary Education*. Greater London Papers No. 11. London School of Economics. *59*

Poignant, R. (1969) *Education and Development in Western Europe, the United States and the USSR*. (English translation.) New York: Teachers College Press. *28, 36, 37*

Price, R. (1970) *Education in Communist China*. London: Routledge and Kegan Paul. *25*

Rosenthal, R. and Jacobson, L. (1968) *Pygmalion in the Classroom*. New York: Holt, Rinehart and Winston. *93, 101*

Rubinstein, D. and Simon, B. (1973) *The Evolution of the Comprehensive School: 1926–1972*. 2nd edition. London: Routledge and Kegan Paul. *60*

Saran, R. (1973) *Policy-Making in Secondary Education: a Case Study.* Oxford University Press. *56*

Simon, B. (1965) *Education and the Labour Movement: 1870–1920.* London: Lawrence and Wishart. *38*

Simon, B. (1970) Egalitarianism versus education. *Comprehensive Education 14*: 5. *19*

Stinchcombe, A. (1964) *Rebellion in a High School.* Chicago: Quadrangle Books. *88*

Swift, D. (1965) Social class and achievement motivation. *Educational Research 8*: 83. *47*

Turner, R. (1961) Modes of ascent through education: sponsored and contest mobility. In A. Halsey *et al.* (ed.) *Education, Economy and Society.* Glencoe, Illinois: Free Press. *42*

Vernon, P. (1956) *The Measurement of Abilities.* 2nd edition. London University Press. *20*

Waller, W. (1965) *The Sociology of Teaching.* New York: Wiley. (Originally published 1932.) *41*

Yates, A. (1968) *Grouping in Education.* New York: Wiley. *100*

Young, D. (1967) Comprehensive schools – the danger of counter-revolution. *Comprehensive Education 5*: 6. *82*

Young, M. F. D. (1971) An approach to the study of curricula as socially organized knowledge. In M. F. D. Young (ed.) *Knowledge and Control.* London: Collier-Macmillan. *33*

Subject index